Reaching Post-Christian Europeans

Bjørn Ottesen

Reaching Post-Christian Europeans

Newbold Academic Press

Author:
   Bjørn Ottesen
Graphic design:
   Any Kobel, Switzerland
Layout:
   CAB Service, Germany
Typesetting:
   Manfred Lemke
Printing:
   INGRAM

©Bjørn Ottesen, 2015

The opinions expressed in our published works are those of the author(s) and do not reflect the opinions of Newbold Academic Press or its Publishing Panel.

Except as otherwise permitted under the Copyright, Designs and Patents Act 1988 this publication may only be reproduced, stored or transmitted in any form or by any means, with the prior permission of the publisher, or in the case of reprographic reproduction, in accordance with the terms of a licence issued by The Copyright Licensing Agency. Enquiries concerning reproduction outside those terms should be sent to Newbold Academic Press, Bracknell, Berkshire, RG42 4AN, UK.

ISBN 978-0-9932188-2-8, Softcover
ISBN 978-0-9932188-3-5, e-Book

Contents

Acknowledgements — 9
Introduction — 11

PART ONE - MINISTRY CONTEXT

CHAPTER 1
Literature review — 17

CHAPTER 2
Changes in Danish culture and society – I — 33

CHAPTER 3
Changes in Danish culture and society – II — 61

CHAPTER 4
The Seventh-day Adventist church in Denmark — 85

PART TWO - THEOLOGICAL REFLECTION

CHAPTER 5
Theological reflection on the church and its mission — 111

CHAPTER 6
Perspectives on change — 135

PART THREE - MINISTRY STRATEGY

CHAPTER 7

Reaching the current Danish poplulation   155

CHAPTER 8

Small group ministry in the Adventist context   167

BIBLIOGRAPHY   189

Acknowledgements

This book is a revised version of my DMin dissertation submitted to Fuller Theological Seminary. Its production has proved to be an exciting academic and spiritual walk. Above all, I would like to thank God for his support and his provision of the strength required to complete the task. Special thanks go to my godly professors at Fuller who have guided and taught me. My best friend and wife, Maj-Britt, has been a wonderful conversation partner throughout. I would like to thank her for her patience during those times when evenings together were postponed in favour of hours of study. I am also indebted to the leadership of the Trans-European Division of the Seventh-day Adventist Churches who sponsored my studies and gave me the opportunity for personal and professional development. Dr. Michael Pearson, supervisor and mentor, has brought a lifetime of teaching experience and academic excellence to our deliberations. Your support, Mike, was invaluable. Finally, thanks go to James Love, Manfred Lemke and Jean-Claude Verrecchia who have proof-read and edited this publication.

Introduction

Immense changes have taken place in Danish society since the Seventh-day Adventist Church (hereafter Adventist Church) started its ministry there in 1878. Some have affected the church significantly. In the 1950s and 1960s people's relationship to traditional Christian values and faith altered dramatically. Within the last twenty years the industrial society of the twentieth century has been replaced by an information society. Public life has become more secular, with few references to religion.

The major shifts in society pose new challenges and opportunities to the Adventist Church. The goal of this study is to analyse recent cultural changes in Danish society and understand how they represent challenges to — and opportunities for — the mission of the Adventist Church. The main thesis of this study is that given the increasing relational and experiential nature of learning and spirituality in Danish culture, local congregations within the Adventist Church will be more fruitful in evangelism if they intentionally develop holistic small groups and networks in which the gospel can be both embodied and proclaimed.

The significance of this study lies in several areas. It will provide useful insights for the leaders and pastors in the Adventist Church in Denmark. Church elders and others in positions of responsibility may also profit from the findings. Since many other denominations face the same issues and challenges as the Adventist Church, the observations, analyses and conclusions reached here may be useful to Christian leaders in other denominations — in Denmark and also beyond its borders.

I have a strong personal interest in finding answers to the questions posed here. When I started work on this study, I was the national leader for the Adventist Church in Denmark. My interest in this topic was for obvious reasons. In the meantime I have accepted another position and am currently teaching ministerial students in a Western European context at Newbold College of Higher Education in England. The insights this study brings will be of importance for the environment where I am now, and also in the many local fields where students later will work. This study will, I trust, contribute to the growth of the kingdom of God and the fulfilment of the mission Jesus Christ gave to his disciples.

The discussion and analysis in this study is based mainly on literature describing recent changes in Danish culture (and Northern European culture in general). It draws lessons from studies of people and society, from both secular and religious points of view. There are lessons from Adventist history and particularly from two local Adventist Churches where growth has been closely connected to a strong personal ministry and the use of networks and small groups.

The study is divided into three parts. Part One concerns the Adventist Church and its Danish context. Chapter 1 provides an overview of significant literature on changes in Danish society and countries with similar cultures. Important insights are given through qualitative and quantitative studies conducted in the Nordic Countries. In addition, some larger European research projects are used as evidence. This chapter reviews literature on the mission of the Adventist Church in Western countries and beyond. There has been only limited research done in Denmark on issues related to the Adventist Church, so this chapter takes into consideration research from countries with similar cultures.

Chapters 2 and 3 give a description of recent changes in Danish society. An attempt is made to describe alterations particularly related to spirituality, faith and religiosity. Furthermore, these chapters analyse how these changes have influenced the population's relationship to Christian faith and to the church.

The purpose of chapter 4 is to provide an introduction to the Adventist Church as a backdrop for the discussion in the following chapters. It makes a short reference to the origins of the movement in the United States, but most attention is given to the work and mission of the Adventist Church in Denmark. This chapter also offers a picture of the current state of the church.

Part Two provides theological reflection on the Universal Church and its mission. Chapter 5 presents a brief theology of church and its mission. Particular reference is given to the topic under consideration in this study: the mission of the Adventist Church in Denmark. Rather than presenting a comprehensive theology of church and mission, the chapter draws lessons from two New Testament books of particular relevance: the book of Acts, because it describes times of great change in the story of God's people, and the Epistle to the Ephesians because of its strong teaching on the church and an individual's relation to Christ and his people. From that platform reflection is offered on how these teachings challenge the Adventist Church's as it takes part in the purposes of God.

Chapter 6 outlines the theological basis for doing incarnational ministry. This chapter will provide examples from the Bible and from the history of the Adventist Church of how the church throughout time has changed some of its practices, values and message in order to do God's will on earth. These changes provide a theological foundation for the acceptance of necessary changes at the present time.

Part Three presents a response to the current mission challenge. Chapter 7 brings the research in the previous chapters together. In an analysis of, and reflection on, these findings conclusions for Adventist ministry are made, with a particular view to methods of evangelism that relate to current trends and needs in society.

Chapter 8 is a practical response to the conclusions in chapter 7. Having demonstrated, among other conclusions, the importance of relationships in evangelism, a practical guide to how small groups and networks of people can function well, is provided. Attention is given to motivation, leadership, organisation and the particulars of the small-group meeting. In addition, this chapter explains how small groups and networks can be a part of the mission of the church in a local community and how they can be used for the benefit of the people in the local church.

This study is not a study on doctrinal issues, but its aim is to suggest practical methods for reaching people with the gospel. It is of considerable importance, however, to think through some of the Adventist Church's teachings and how they can be reapplied in today's time.

This study does not discuss at length issues of church policy, authority, structures or membership. It is both relevant and necessary for the church, as an organisation, to discuss these practices in light of the mentality of current times. However, in the context of this study these issues are only touched on briefly.

There are aspects of the cultural shift in Denmark which will be given only a brief mention, but which are of significance nevertheless. These are factors such as living standards, consumerism, the welfare state, educational opportunities, life expectancy, health issues and new communication forms, which all have an impact on individuals and society as a whole. They are referred to in the text, but not in depth. In this study the intention is to look closely at those issues which are most relevant to religious faith, spirituality and relationship to the church.

The focus on small groups and networks does not cover all that could be said about evangelism in Denmark today. In light of the diversity of needs in cultures, groups and individuals, there is room for a multiplicity of methods in evangelism. The central claim in this book, however, is that most methods are strongest in combination with a personal ministry in which relationships, networks and small groups are major elements in the evangelism and discipleship processes.

PART ONE
MINISTRY CONTEXT

CHAPTER 1

Literature review

The gradual changes in the Danish religious scenery over the last half-a-century have become more obvious the last twenty years. The number of people who have religious commitments is falling. Intuitively church leaders and workers know that the future will be very different from the past, and the question is asked whether they are facing the demise of Christianity and church-related faith. On the other hand, Christianity could just be making adjustments to a new era where the content and structures of faith, organisations and lifestyles are different. Radical changes have happened in the life of the Church before. This study will describe and analyse some recent changes in Danish society, particularly relating to faith and religion.

It will look at a series of quantitative and qualitative studies which document clear changes in faith and religious practice. On this basis the consequences for the Church, particularly the Adventist Church, will be analysed. The first part of this chapter will introduce significant research projects which document changes in faith and religious practice. These studies are from Denmark, other Nordic countries and Europe. Significant attempts have been made by the Adventist Church and other churches to understand and respond to the changing religious scenery. The second part of this chapter looks at some of these responses from within the Church. There is a particular emphasis on literature from the Adventist Church. Conferences have been held and literature written to grapple with the new trends. This study's primary focus is to identify and develop a ministry model for spiritual growth and discipleship in the new spiritual environment. Therefore some significant literature on ministry models will be referred to in the third part of this chapter.

Current Changes in Society

Issues related to secularism, individualism, pluralism, postmodernism and a new spirituality are particularly relevant to the discussion of changes in faith and spirituality. Steve Bruce has written several volumes on secularisation from a non-Christian point of view. His volume *God is Dead: Secularisation in the West*,[1] is particularly interesting for this research. Bruce's arguments are challenged by Grace Davie in *Europe: The Exceptional Case*.[2] Erik Bjerager, chief editor for the Danish Christian national newspaper *Kristelig Dagblad*, writes specifically about the secularisation process of Denmark in his volume *Gud Bevare Danmark: et Opgør Med Secularismen*[3] [*God Save Denmark: A Showdown on Secularism*].

Scandinavian literature specifically dealing with postmodernism is limited, but the issue is touched on by several authors quoted in chapter 3. Internationally, Christian authors respond in different ways. Among those who see postmodern thinking as a threat to Christianity is D. A. Carson, who expresses his concerns in *Becoming Conversant with the Emerging Church*.[4] Stanley J. Grenz advocates a sceptical approach in *A Primer on Postmodernism*.[5] In contrast some Christian writers remind the reader that Christianity did not arise in

---

[1] Steve Bruce, *God Is Dead: Secularisation in the West* (Oxford: Blackwell, 2002).2002
[2] Grace Davie, *Europe: The Exceptional Case* (London: Darton Longman & Todd, 2002).
[3] Erik Bjerager, *Gud Bevare Danmark - et Opgør Med Secularismen* (Gylling: Gyldendal, 2006).
[4] D. A. Carson, *Becoming Conversant with the Emerging Church: Understanding a Movement and its Implications* (Grand Rapids, MI: Zondervan, 2005).
[5] Stanley J. Grenz, *A Primer on Postmodernism* (Grand Rapids, MI: Eerdmans, 1996).

a "modern" context, but in pre-modern times. They suggest that the postmodern worldview might have more in common with original Christian thinking than the modern church would like to accept. In this category would be Crystal Downing in *How Postmodernism Serves (my) Faith*,[6] John D. Caputo in *What Would Jesus Deconstruct?*,[7] and James K.A. Smith in *Who's Afraid of Postmodernism?*[8]

Some Scandinavian volumes present research on the new age Movement and a new spirituality. Two works by Lars Ahlin are noted here: *Pilgrim, Turist eller Flykting*, [*Pilgrim, Tourist, or Refugee*][9] and his article written with co-authors 'Religious Diversity and Pluralism'.[10] Olav Hammer has described how the Danish population is affected by a new spirituality in *På Jagt Efter Helheden: New Age - En Ny Folketro*[11] [*The Search for the Wholistic: new age – a New Folklore*]. Grace Davie, Linda Woodhead and Paul Heelas have explored similar territory in England. Their findings were published in *Predicting Religion: Christian, Secular, and Alternative Futures*.[12]

The present largest research project in Denmark on changes in faith, spirituality and religion, is "The Pluralism Project."[13] The project is managed in an interdisciplinary fashion between departments at

---

[6] Crystal Downing, *How Postmodernism Serves (my) Faith: Questioning Truth in Language, Philosophy and Art* (Downers Grove, IL: InterVarsity Press Academic, 2006).

[7] John D. Caputo, *What Would Jesus Deconstruct? The Good News of Postmodernism for the Church* (Grand Rapids, MI: Baker Academic, 2007).

[8] James K. A Smith, *Who's Afraid of Postmodernism? Taking Derrida, Lyotard, and Foucault to Church* (Grand Rapids, MI: Baker Academic, 2006).

[9] Lars Ahlin, *Pilgrim, Turist eller Flykting? en studie av individuell religiös rörlighet i senmoderniteten* (Stockholm: Östlings bokförlag Symposion, 2005).

[10] Lars Ahlin et al., 'Religious Diversity and Pluralism: Empirical Data and Theoretical Reflection from the Danish Pluralism Project', *Journal of Contemporary Religion*, 27:3 (October 2012), 403–18.

[11] Olav Hammer, *På Jagt Efter Helheden: New Age - En Ny Folketro* (Aarhus: Clemenstrykkeriet, 1997).

[12] Grace Davie, Linda Woodhead and Paul Heelas, *Predicting Religion: Christian, Secular, and Alternative Futures* (Aldershot: Ashgate, 2003).

[13] Marianne C. Qvortrup Fibiger, 'The Danish Pluralism Project', *Religion*, 39:2 (2009), 169–75.

the University of Aarhus. When the project first started in 2002, research was carried out only in Aarhus, the second largest city in Denmark. The expanded project has grown and provides insights into the changing religious scene in all of Denmark. Some of the observations appear to be devastating to traditional Christianity and Church organisations. According to the findings the institutions of modernism have little relevance to people's spirituality today. People define their own spiritual walk independent of any authority and freely mix elements from different spiritual traditions and thought systems to make up a spirituality which suits them. The institutional Church has lost its traditional place in the life of the Danish population. The findings raises serious questions about the form in which Christian faith will continue to have influence, or indeed, if it will survive at all. Some of the findings of the Pluralism Project and the consequences for the Church will be discussed further in the following chapters. Peter Gundelach, Hans Iversen and Margit Warburgh did a qualitative study interviewing thirty-four Danes on issues of faith. The conclusions published in *I hjertet af Danmark*[14] [*In the Heart of Denmark*] confirm the above. Danes make up their own content for their faith. The typical relationship to the Church is expressed by one interviewee: 'We are Christians, but we do whatever we like'.[15]

A large quantitative study was carried out among the priests in the Danish National Church the first five years after the turn of the century. The study surveys many aspects of the life, opinions and the work situations of priests. It also summarises how priests in the Danish National Church perceive current trends in Danish society. The findings correspond closely with the research done in The Pluralism Project. Priests see secularisation and "the mixing of religions" as the greatest threats to the Church. The conclusions from the study among

---

[14] Peter Gundelach, Hans Iversen and Margit Warburgh, *I hjertet af Danmark: institutioner og mentaliteter* (Copenhagen: Hans Reitzel, 2008).

[15] Ibid., pp. 136–137.

the priests were published in *Karma, Koran og Kirke*[16] (*Karma, Koran and Church*) in 2007, and are discussed further in chapters 2 and 3.

Three qualitative studies that describe changes in the thinking of the younger generations in Scandinavians have been carried out by Inger Furseth, Paul Otto Brunstad and Erling Birkedal. Though conducted in Norway, they carry significance for the study of changes in the Danish mentality. The ways of life in Denmark and Norway are very similar as the two countries share a long history of common rule and language, and have strong ties through trade, intermarriage and tourism. Furseth interviewed people of different generations on issues relating to faith, religion, relationships, group membership and their relationship to the Church. Her research demonstrates dramatic changes in how individuals relate to themselves and to the groups they are part of. Two are particularly important. First, younger generations tend to see faithfulness to their genuine self as the ultimate value. Second, groups are interesting to the individual only as they contribute to the development of oneself. These attitudes challenge the Church and are explored in chapter 2. Furseth's findings are published in *From Quest for Truth to Being Oneself*.[17]

In the 1990s Paul Otto Brunstad carried out a qualitative study on seventy young people aged sixteen to nineteen. He interviewed them on issues relating to faith and Church finding that spirituality was on the increase and challenged the idea that people are becoming increasingly secular. Immediately this could be interpreted as positive for the Christian Church, but on closer inspection difficulties emerge. The new spirituality does not seem to be determined by the teachings of the Church, but by individual choices where each person constructs his or her own faith system. Individuality is encouraged and seen as the authentic option. Brunstad also shows that a strong

---

[16] Berit Schelde Christensen, Viggo Mortensen and Lars Buch Viftrup, *Karma, Koran Og Kirke; Religiøs Mangfoldighed Som Folkekirkelig Udfordring* (Højbjerg: Forlaget Univers, 2007).

[17] Inger Furseth, *From Quest for Truth to Being Oneself* (Frankfurt: Peter Lang, 2006).

factor leading a young person to identify with a certain set of beliefs is the relationship to a significant person who carries these beliefs. Brunstad's research was published in *Ungdom and Livstolkning* [*Youth and Interpretation of Life*].[18]

Erling Birkedal's study, conducted in Norway, is of a similar nature to those of Brunstad and Furseth, and is published in *Noen Ganger tror jeg på Gud*[19] [*Sometimes I Believe in God*]. This study is concerned solely with young people and their relationship to faith, religion and those relationships in which faith is lived and expressed. He describes a strong individuality which challenges adherence to any doctrinal belief system or faith organisation.

A quantitative study worth attention is Anders Sjöborg's research on Swedish people's relationship to the Bible, comparing findings from 1984 and 2000. (Again, Swedish culture is close to Danish and the same reasons apply to Norwegian culture.) This research was done as a PhD project at Uppsala University and was published as *Bibeln på mina Egna Villkor*[20] [*The Bible on My Own Terms*].

There are three large European quantitative studies which deal with a whole series of demographic issues relevant to this study. These longitudinal studies have been repeated from the 1980s to the present time and include statistical data from Denmark. One such study is *Religious and Moral Pluralism* (*RAMP*) which is a European research project covering twelve countries. Research into the same issues has been repeated for the last thirty years, thus creating a nuanced picture of developments. The findings for the Nordic countries have been published in *Folkkyrkor Och Religiös Pluralism: Den Nordiska*

---

[18] Paul Otto Brunstad, *Ungdom Og Livstolkning* (Trondheim: Tapir forlag, 1998).
[19] Erling Birkedal, *Noen Ganger Tror Jeg På Gud, Men* (Trondheim: Forlaget Tapir, 2001).
[20] Anders Sjöborg, *Bibeln På Mina Egna Villkor* (Uppsala: Uppsala University Library, 2006).

Religiösa Modellen[21] [*National Churches and Religious Pluralism: The Nordic Model*]. The second study is *The European Values Study (EVS)*,[22] a research project undertaken between 1981 and 2008 in eleven European countries. The results for Denmark are summarised in *Små og Store Forandringer* [*Small and Large Changes*].[23] Peter Ester also draws conclusions from *EVS* for Denmark in *The Individualizing Society*.[24] *EVS* has provided results corresponding to those of *RAMP*. The third European study is *The European Social Study (ESS)*. Some significant findings from *ESS* for the Danish context are found in *Fremtidens Danske Religionsmodel* [*A Future Danish Religious Model*].[25] These comprehensive surveys document significant changes in the patterns of religious practice, values and faith in the European population. The findings of particular interest for the Danish situation will be analysed in the following chapters.

Reflections and Responses from the Church

It should be noted that, generally, there has been limited research done within the Adventist Church in Scandinavian countries. The churches are small, with relatively few members, and few resources have been devoted to this purpose. In Europe, more generally some significant work has been done to try to understand the church's role in the new spiritual setting and some authors have produced noteworthy books and articles.

---

[21] Göran Gustafsson (ed.), *Folkkyrkor Och Religiös Pluralism: Den Nordiska Religiösa Modellen* (Stockholm: Verbum, 2000).

[22] European Values Study, 'The European Values Study', http://www.europeanvaluesstudy.eu/, EuropeanValuesStudy.eu (accessed 10 August 2013).

[23] Peter Gundelach, *Smaa og store Forandringer: Danskernes Værdier siden 1981* (Copenhagen: Hans Reitzels Forlag, 2011).

[24] Peter Ester, *The Individualizing Society* (Tilburg: Tilburg University Press, 1994).

[25] Referred to in Lisbeth Christoffersen et al., *Fremtidens Danske Religionsmodel* (Copenhagen: Forlaget Anis, 2012).

Reinder Bruinsma is one influential Adventist author who has closely examined, written and lectured extensively on the changes in European culture. Having worked on several continents as a pastor, teacher and church administrator, he has made postmodern culture a particular emphasis in his writing and teaching over the last one-and-a-half decades. His contributions are variously referred to in other chapters in this study.

Bruinsma has tried to challenge the Adventist Church to face up to recent changes in society. He has aspired to explain some of the characteristics of the new culture, and suggested ways of presenting the gospel and the Adventist message in new and relevant formats. Some of Bruinsma's contributions include his books on Adventist faith, expressed in a new fashion such as *It's Time to Stop Rehearsing What We Believe & Start Looking at What Difference It Makes*.[26] His more recent book, *Faith Step by Step: Finding God and Yourself*, may be even more significant.[27] Bruinsma's writings include a number of articles[28] on postmodernism and other factors that tend to challenge the Adventist Church today. While he has taught extensively on Adventist College campuses and at pastors' gatherings, his expansive work has not changed patterns of operation significantly in local churches.

Another leader in the Adventist Church in Europe who has done significant work in this area, is Miroslav Pujic, who is himself a graduate of Fuller Theological Seminary. Stationed at the headquarters of the

---

[26] Reinder Bruinsma, *It's Time to Stop Rehearsing What We Believe & Start Looking at What Difference It Makes* (Nampa, ID: Pacific Press, 1998).

[27] Reinder Bruinsma, *Faith Step by Step: Finding God and Yourself* (Grantham: Stanborough Press, 2006).

[28] Representative of Bruinsma's many contributions are three articles: Reinder Bruinsma, 'Modern Versus Postmodern Adventism: The Ultimate Divide?', *Ministry Magazine*, 77:6 (2005), 16; Reinder Bruinsma, 'Adventist Identity in a Postmodern World', *Spectrum*, 41:2 (Spring 2013), 32; and Bruinsma's chapter, 'Is the Postmodern Adventist a Threat to the Unity of his Church?' in *Exploring the Frontiers of Faith, Festschrift in Honour of Dr. Jan Paulsen*, Børge Schantz and Reinder Bruinsma, eds. (Lueneburg: Advent-Verlag, 2009), p. 75.

Trans-European Division[29] (TED) of the Adventist Church, Pujic has taught pastors and students throughout Europe and beyond. For a time he headed the work of the Centre for Secular & Postmodern Studies – an institute set up by the General Conference (world headquarters) of the Adventist Church. When it comes to publications, Pujic's main contribution has been a series of evangelistic materials under the umbrella heading of Life Development. The Adventist Church in Great Britain invested more than a million pounds in the development of this material which included Bible studies, videos, small-group materials and explanations of a discipleship track.[30] Pujic has encouraged the Adventist Church to take brave steps to connect with new generations which have worldviews and lifestyles different from the traditional Christian ways, by trying to explain the thinking of these new generations.[31]

Yet there has been a breach in the link between the brainpower that created a new philosophy of ministry and created the material to go with it, and the people who would actually use the material in local settings. For the many non-English speaking countries in TED, there were challenges of translation and editing. For the large Adventist Church in the United Kingdom, Life Development failed to catch on. One can speculate as to whether the concept was perceived as a postmodern white project imposing something on a predominantly modern black church. Some indicate that the introduction of the programme to the British Church failed because of lack of communication. The Church in Britain might want to analyse why this huge investment did not bring a better result.

---

[29] The Trans European Division of the Adventist Church is the headquarters for the churches in 22 European countries.
[30] This material can be seen at www.lifedevelopment.info. See also Miroslav Pujic and Sarah K. Asaftei, *Experiencing the Joy* (St. Albans: LIFEdevelopment Discipleship Library, 2012).
[31] One example is: Miroslav Pujic, 'Postmodern Cultural Patterns', *Ministry Magazine,* 85:6 (June 2013), 30.

Two collections of articles by other Adventist scholars deserve mention here. Though some years have passed since their publication, they represent forward thinking and serious research. Sadly, the insights from these volumes do not appear to have been read or received by a significant number of pastors and members in the European churches. The first volume, *Casting the Net on the Right Side*,[32] is the compilation of proceedings of a symposium in Freudenstadt, Germany in 1991. The volume described a number of "-isms" facing the Church. The entries on new age spirituality, pluralism and secularism are of particular interest to this paper.

The second collection of articles from the Adventist Church is the outcome of a conference on mission, held in the Netherlands in 1997, involving church leaders and scholars from Europe and the US. The presentations were published in *Re-Visioning Adventist Mission in Europe*.[33] This larger volume also includes reflections on current changes in faith and spirituality in Europe, and on the consequences for the Church. Some articles move on to suggested methods for evangelism in the current climate.

Reflecting on the work of Bruinsma, Pujic and the two mentioned publications, it has proven difficult to bring the many ideas and reflections from an intellectual elite to the local pastors and the local church members throughout Europe. This may indicate a crucial disconnect between thinkers and doers in the Adventist Church. It may also reflect the fact that it is easier to share philosophical and ideologically controversial ideas in an environment where there are a majority of intellectuals. Even more likely, there has been a breakdown in strategy for communicating the new ideas.

---

[32] Richard Lehmann, Jack Mahon and Børge Schantz, eds., *Cast the Net on the Right Side: Seventh-day Adventists Face the "Isms"* (Bracknell: European Institute of World Mission, 1993).

[33] Erich Walter Baumgartner, *Re-Visioning Adventist Mission in Europe* (Berrien Springs, MI: Andrews University Press, 1998).

Changes in thinking and ideology which have taken intellectuals months and years to elaborate, are not going to be accepted in local churches overnight. In addition to strategies for communicating new ideas to members, programmes and procedures which establish new patterns of behaviour and operation must be implemented. Kjell Aune, writing on the situation of the Adventist Church in Norway, comments on the need for the leadership of conferences and local churches to work together on a strategic approach to evangelism. In his DMin study *A Contextual Analysis of the Seventh-day Adventist Church in Norway*,[34] Aune advocates a strong emphasis on method, strategy and coordinated planning. His work mentions many of the changes in attitudes in the general population, but the sensitive issues of the need for change in the Adventist Church are not discussed in detail.

Little is written by Christian Scandinavian authors specifically on evangelism in the new cultural setting. The Lutheran National Churches, which dominate the Scandinavian countries as far as membership is concerned, seem to have a less than urgent relationship with evangelism. One volume worth mentioning would be the DAWN report published as *Gør Danerne Kristne*[35] [*Make the Danes Christian*], which outlines some evangelistic strategies from an Evangelical/ Pentecostal point of view. However, there are some major social studies, as seen above, which describe changes in people's

---

[34] Kjell Aune, *A Contextual Analysis of the Seventh-day Adventist Church in Norway: with Suggestions for Renewal and Growth*, DMin Dissertation (Berrien Springs, MI: Andrews University Theological Seminary, 2005). Aune's conclusions in relation to church growth are similar to the conclusions of this study. The following quote is from the Abstract of the dissertation (no page): 'Church growth is not just something technical, functional or numerical. It is a project of the heart. Outer growth starts with inner growth. Based on demographics of the Norwegian society, it can be concluded that there is a neeed for home-based, relational and felt-need activities. The church needs to be more sensitive towards the needs and ways of postmoderns and youth. More variety and tolerance is called for.'

[35] Søren Roulund-Nørgaard, *Gør danerne kristne: DAWN rapporten* (Aalborg: SALT, 1992).

faith and spirituality. This study will attempt to establish methods of evangelism based on these documented descriptions of the current population in Denmark.

The Adventist Church in Denmark

The history of the worldwide Adventist Church has been outlined by several authors. George Knight is the most prolific contemporary observer of the tradition. His volumes *William Miller and the Rise of Adventism*[36] and *A Brief History of Seventh-day Adventists*[37] are informative about the church's beginnings in the US. Knight's book on the development of Adventist thought, *A Search for Identity: The Development of Seventh-Day Adventist Beliefs*,[38] is a helpful overview. Other volumes on Adventist history and thought development are C. Mervyn Maxwell's *Tell It to the World*,[39] Richard W. Schwarz's *Light Bearers to the Remnant*,[40] P. Gerard Damsteegt's *Foundations of the Seventh-day Adventist Message and Mission*,[41] and Leroy Edwin Froom's *Movement of Destiny*.[42] These volumes tend to see the history of the Adventist Church from an internal perspective. That is also true of the limited literature about the history of the Adventist Church in Denmark. Hans Jørgen Schantz has written about significant people in the history of the Danish Church in *I Troens Bagspejl*[43] [*In the Rear*

---

[36] George R. Knight, *William Miller and the Rise of Adventism* (Nampa, ID: Pacific Press, 2011).

[37] George R. Knight, *A Brief History of Seventh-day Adventists* (Hagesrstown, MD: Review & Herald, 2012).

[38] George R Knight, *A Search for Identity: The Development of Seventh-Day Adventist Beliefs* (Hagerstown, MD: Review & Herald, 2000).

[39] C. Mervyn Maxwell, *Tell It to the World* (Boise, ID: Pacific Press, 1998).

[40] Richard W. Schwarz, *Light Bearers to the Remnant: Denominational History Textbook for Seventh-Day Adventist College Classes* (Mountain View, CA: Pacific Press, 1979).

[41] P. Gerard Damsteegt, *Foundations of the Seventh-day Adventist Message and Mission* (Berrien Springs, MI: Andrews University Press, 1995).

[42] Leroy Edwin Froom, *Movement of Destiny* (Washington, DC: Review & Herald, 1971).

[43] Hans Jørgen Schantz, *I Troens Bakspejl* (Copenhagen: Dansk Bogforlag, 1998).

Mirror of Faith]. More recently Kaj Pedersen published *Syvende-dags Adventistkirken i Danmark* [44] [*The Adventist Church in Denmark*]. The archives of the Adventist Church (HASDA) have proved a valuable source.[45]

Ministry

This study identifies small groups, networks and relationships as significant for evangelism in the emerging spiritual environment. A similar conclusion was reached by Allan Roy Walshe in his DMin study for Fuller Theological Seminary, an analysis of the needs of the Adventist Church in New Zealand. Even if New Zealand is on the opposite side of the globe from Denmark, the culture there has a lot in common with European culture. In *A Paradigm Shift: Moving from an Informational to a Relational Model of Ministry in the Adventist Churches of New Zealand*,[46] Walshe challenges the traditional Adventist approach to evangelism dominated by the presentation of propositional truth and information. He demonstrates the need for a relational approach to evangelism in the current social environment.

As small groups and relationships will emerge as significant in evangelism, some resources on that topic need consideration. One of the pioneering organisations which introduced more relational Bible studies for groups was Serendipity which, since the early-1980s, has generated a flow of relational material. The Serendipity approach to fellowship around biblical texts has been paving a way for a new strategy in regard to Bible study. Now there is a wealth of materials on small groups, so much so that it is hard to select particular works for mention here. However, two books from Willow Creek have been

---

[44] Kaj Pedersen, *Syvende Dags Adventistkirken i Danmark* (Copenhagen: Dansk Bogforlag, 2007).

[45] HASDA, 'HASDA home page', http://haAdventist.dk/Default. aspx?ID=10971 (accessed 20 March 2014).

[46] Allan Roy Walshe, *A Paradigm Shift: Moving from an Informational to a Relational Model of Ministry in the Adventist Churches of New Zealand*, DMin dissertation (Pasadena, CA: Fuller Theological Seminary, 2007).

helpful in describing how to use relationships and small groups as evangelistic tools: Bill Donahue's *Building a Church of Small Groups*[47] and Garry Poole's *Seeker Small Groups*.[48]

Two recent, and important, trends within Christianity are the "emerging church" and the "missional church."[49] Representatives of these two expressions of church have written on mission and evangelism. Some suggest ministry models which work in a postmodern context. One volume that describes new ministry models is Eddie Gibbs and Ryan Bolger's *Emerging Churches*.[50] Another helpful volume is *Missional Church* edited by Darrell Guder,[51] which is more a theology of Church than a practical guide to ministry. Michael Frost and Allan Hirsh have challenged traditional church ministry through *The Shaping of Things to Come* and *The Forgotten Ways* in which new ministry models are suggested. Although written in an Australian or North American context, these books convey ideas of interest also for churches in Western Europe.

There are qualitative and quantitative studies done in Denmark and Scandinavia that describe changing patterns in people's relationship to faith, spirituality, religion and Church. There is limited literature, however, from within the Church on mission and evangelism. Pastors in churches with an evangelistic approach tend to rely on intuition and methods suiting their own personalities. New methods are being

---

[47] Bill Donahue, *Building a Church of Small Groups: A Place Where Nobody Stands Alone* (Grand Rapids, MI: Zondervan, 2001).

[48] Garry Poole, *Seeker Small Groups: Engaging Spiritual Seekers in Life-changing Discussions* (Grand Rapids, MI: Zondervan : Willow Creek Resources, 2003).

[49] Emerging church often refers to church plants which operate in a manner that suits the postmodern person. Missional church refers to a pattern of thinking which sees mission and evangelism as the sole reason for the existence of the church, rather than being one activity among many in church life.

[50] Eddie Gibbs and Ryan Bolger, *Emerging Churches: Creating Christian Communities in Postmodern Cultures* (Grand Rapids, MI: Baker Academic, 2005).

[51] Darrell L Guder, ed., *Missional Church: A Vision for the Sending of the Church in North America* (Grand Rapids, MI: Eerdmans, 1998).

tested. This study contributes to filling this gap through an analysis of the present trends in the population, connects that to a theological reflection, and establishes how that knowledge points towards certain approaches and practices.

CHAPTER 2

Changes in Danish culture and society – I

The following two chapters provide an account of recent changes in the lifestyle, values, faith, mindset and relationships of Danes. This account helps assess how these changes affect the mission and the evangelistic methods of the Adventist Church. Chapter 3 differs by specifically focusing on "postmodernism" and "a new spirituality."

A Changing Danish Culture

In the late-nineteenth century Denmark was an agrarian society. The large majority of the population lived in the countryside, owned a piece of land and were, to a large extent, self-sufficient. But because of growing industrialisation, some cities were already increasing in sise. The early mission of the Adventist Church was mainly to address the people living in small villages and communities throughout this farming landscape. Almost all of the population were members of the National Lutheran Church. Almost all Danes were baptised as children and had a basic Christian faith. Most people had an understanding and knowledge of fundamental Christian beliefs about God, Jesus, the Bible, the Lord's Prayer, the confessions of the Church, the Ten Commandments and Christian ethics. This does not mean that everyone was a believer or that there were uniform ideas about religion and faith; the Enlightenment had produced a religious ferment in Denmark.

On the religious scene, a significant change occurred when Denmark implemented a new constitution in 1848. Up to that time, there had been an increasing number of incidents and questions related to various religious practices. These involved Jews and other specific immigrant groups such as French and Dutch merchants and farmers who were invited to enter the country and contribute to Danish society.[1] There were particularly serious issues with the Baptists. Many Baptists had been penalised for not baptising their children. Baptist preachers had been fined or imprisoned for preaching and baptising without the consent and recognition of the State Church. This changed, however, with the introduction of the new constitution. People were given freedom in their practice of faith. The National Church was nevertheless granted a unique position as a church and it was still regarded as an official agent of the government, functioning along with the legislative, judicial and executive agencies.[2]

From the mid-nineteenth century until the mid-twentieth century Denmark developed from a rural, agricultural society into a more urban, industrial one. As industry and farming became more and more mechanised, resources continued to be released for other priorities. Denmark metamorphosed from a production economy to a service economy, and specifically over the last twenty years Denmark has moved from an industrial society to an information society. People have migrated in increasing numbers from the countryside to cities, educational levels have increased and people's living standards and sense of independence have also risen. These social changes have taken place in most Western European countries and are described and documented elsewhere.[3] This chapter and the next are focused on general trends among the indigenous majority of the

---

[1] Belonging to the Dutch reformed, French reformed or Catholic Church.

[2] Viggo Mortensen, *Kristendommen Under Forvandling* (Højbjerg: Forlaget Univers, 2005), p. 25.

[3] There are numerous volumes describing the changes that took place in European society from the middle of the 1800s up to present time. Three examples are: T.C.V. Blanning (ed.), *The Oxford Illustrated History of Modern Europe* (New York: Oxford University Press, 1996), H. Hearder,

population. The main goal is to describe some of the changes, specific to Danes, in spirituality, faith and relationship to the Church. Thus the issues highlighted are secularisation, individualism, pluralism, postmodernism and a new spirituality.[4]

Secularisation

The secularisation of society takes place on several levels and has various aspects. When applied to society as a whole, it means that religion has a declining place in public life.[5] There is little or no reference to anything divine or supernatural in the public media, official ceremonies, institutions and public events. When it comes to defining individuals as secular, the meaning is that such people live their lives without regard to a divine power or spiritual force. This is characterised by a lack of traditional religious acts like prayer, worship, Bible reading and church attendance. This section examines secularisation, both from a social and an individual point of view.

Europe in the Nineteenth Century, 1830-1880 (Burnt Mill: Longman, 1988) and J. M. Roberts, *Europe: 1880-1945* (Burnt Mill: Longman, 1989).

[4] Society has changed on many levels. Some other changes that might have been valuable to study are the new ethnic makeup of the Danish population, especially in larger cities. For example, the immigration of a significant number of Muslim people has raised issues of faith and religion in Denmark. For some information on Muslims in Denmark see Tim Jensen, 'Organiseret religion og religionspolitik i Danmark [Organised religion and religion politics in Denmark]', in *Forandringer Af Betydning [Significant Change]*, ed. Dominique Bouchet (Aarhus: Forlaget Afveje, 2009). Muslims in Denmark in 2009 numbered 205,000 (3.8 percent of the general population). Of these 25 percent regularly attended the Mosque. There were 115 mosques in Denmark in 2009. Another important issue is current youth culture, which is changing faster than the culture of the general population.

[5] David Martin, *Religious and the Secular* (London: Routledge & Kegan Paul PLC, 1969). For a detailed discussion of the term "secular," see chapter 4. Anthony Campolo also discusses this at length in his book: *A Reasonable Faith: Responding to Secularism* (Waco, TX: Word Books, 1984), pp. 15-48.

Denmark is often described as one of the most secularised countries in the world.[6] Church attendance is very low and the role of the Church in society is insignificant. There is little reference to religion in public life. In spite of this, belief in the supernatural and the transcendent by the general population and a quest for personal spirituality are both still strong. Research shows that religious beliefs have changed in content, but the number of people who believe in a god stay more or less the same.

The European Values Study[7] (a large secular study of 47 countries in Europe, mainly sponsored by the universities of these countries, hereafter *EVS*) provides detailed insight into the Danish population's relationship to several aspects of religion. The Danish data from the study have been summarised and discussed in *Små og Store Forandringer*. Chapter Four, by Peter Andersen and Peter Lüchau, is of particular relevance as it deals with issues relating to religion between 1981 and 2008.[8] The number of people who did not believe in God in 2008 stood unchanged since 1981, at 22 percent. The number who described themselves as "doubters" had actually fallen from 24 to 19 percent. The percentage of those who believed in a personal God fell from 27 to 22 percent. Most notably, the study shows that the number who answered that they believe in God as a "special spiritual power" increased from 27 to 35 percent in the same period.[9] In view of this it is not true to say that the Danes as individuals were

---

[6] Lisbeth Christoffersen et al., *Fremtidens Danske Religionsmodel* [*A Future Danish Religious Model*] (Copenhagen: Forlaget Anis, 2012), p. 340.

[7] This study was done every nine years from 1981 to 2008. From the beginning this study included eleven European countries, but that number had risen to forty-seven by 2008. It covers issues related to life, family, work, religion, politics and society. The project is mainly sponsored by the universities of the countries that participate.

[8] Peter Gundelach, *Smaa og store Forandringer: Danskernes Værdier siden 1981* [*Changes Small and Large: Danish Values Since 1981*] (Copenhagen: Hans Reitzels Forlag, 2011), p. 76. Gundelach works in the Department of Sociology at the University of Copenhagen and is a member of the "Council of programme directors" in the *EVS*.

[9] Gundelach, *Smaa og store Forandringer*, p. 83.

more secular in 2008 than thirty years earlier. On an individual level, faith and spirituality seemed to be stronger than before.[10] The Danes adjusted their understanding of God in this period, and became more selective about what religious beliefs they wanted to hold.

There is a tension between some of the findings of the *EVS*. On one hand people clearly saw themselves more as believers in 2008 than in 1981. However they developed a different type of faith. On the other hand, Danes saw themselves as being less religious in 2008 than in 1981.[11] These trends point in the direction of an individualised faith, independent of religious organisations. Many Danes seem to define their own faith. They tend to pick the ideas in the Christian faith that fit their liking, and mix these ideas with other religious concepts.

More people believed, by 2008, in "positive" doctrines like "life after death" and fewer believed in "negative" doctrines like "sin." According to the *European Social Survey*[12] (hereafter *ESS*), although 84 percent of the population were members of the National Church in 2002, when asked about their religious affiliation, only 54 percent placed themselves in the category "Protestant Christianity."[13] This indicates that people may be members of the National Church but have beliefs that differ from its official teachings. Another point of tension, is that church attendance was low and falling in regard to Sunday worship, but growing at the time of festivals like Christmas. This pattern indicates that people do not necessarily identify fully with the church, but use its services at occasion to express their own spirituality.

---

[10] Ibid., p. 85.
[11] Ibid., p. 83.
[12] *The European Social Survey (ESS)* is an academically driven cross-national survey that has been conducted every two years across Europe since 2001. EuropeanSocialSurvey.org, http://www.europeansocialsurvey.org/about/index.html (accessed 9 April 2014).
[13] Christoffersen et al., *Fremtidens Danske Religionsmodel*, p. 119.

According to *EVS*, Danes had more respect for the Church in 2008 than in 1981.[14] At the same time they felt free to "do religion" in their own way. Gundelach writes, 'The religious faith that means something to the Danes, does not necessarily have anything to do with the traditional Christian God, but, rather, it is disconnected from Church, or at least not related to Christian authority'.[15] In one sense, Church has become more important, but people's relationship to it is now defined in a different way. The Danes have not become more secular, but have a different faith.[16] This seems to correspond with a trend in some other European countries.

Davie, as she reflects on the *EVG (EVS)* statistics, states, 'Indeed it seems to me considerably more accurate to suggest that West Europeans remain, by and large, unchurched populations rather than simply secular'.[17] She goes on to say that 'as the institutional disciplines decline, belief not only persists, but becomes increasingly personal, detached and heterogeneous - particularly among young people. The data from the most recent *European Values Study* (1999/2000) strongly reinforce this point'.[18]

In a qualitative study conducted by the University of Copenhagen, thirty-four individuals were interviewed on questions of faith, spirituality and the Church. The conclusions confirm the above: Danes make up the content of their own faith. The typical relationship to the Church is expressed by one interviewee: 'We are Christians, but we do whatever we like'.[19]

---

[14] Gundelach, *Smaa og store forandringer*, p. 89.
[15] Ibid., p. 91.
[16] Ibid., p. 94.
[17] Grace Davie, *Europe: The Exceptional Case* (London: Darton Longman & Todd, 2002), p. 5.
[18] Davie, *Europe.*, p. 8.
[19] Peter Gundelach, Hans Iversen and Margit Warburgh, *I hjertet af Danmark: institutioner og mentaliteter* (Copenhagen: Hans Reitzel, 2008), pp. 136–137.

This observation is given further support by several studies. A Norwegian, Paul Otto Brunstad, carried out a study on young people's relationship to faith and Church in the late-1990s. It was a qualitative study of seventy young people in the age group 16 to 19. Brunstad points this out the following:

> For a long time one could think of this process [of secularisation] as a linear and irreversible development towards an increasingly rational and de-sacralised society without space or need for religion. In the recent debate there have been raised questions as to whether this is correct. . . . For even if institutionalised religion to a large extent has lost its power to influence and control, that does not mean that religion as such has disappeared—rather the opposite; it can appear as if the Western world is experiencing a religious renaissance. [translation mine][20]

Brunstad argues that there is still strong interest in the spiritual on an individual level.[21] Stuart Murray has presented a thorough study of the phenomenon of "Christendom" (by which he means the hundreds of years during which the Church had a position of influence and power in society) and how the Western world seems to have moved into "post-Christendom." In his book *Church after Christendom* he makes an observation similar to Brunstad's above: 'Few people doubt the influence of secularity, but many detect a countertrend of

---

[20] Paul Otto Brunstad, *Ungdom Og Livstolkning* [*Youth and Interpretation of Life*] (Trondheim, NO: Tapir forlag, 1998), p. 27. This almost 300-page document deserves much more attention than can be given here because it offers deep insights into the thinking of young people in Scandinavia, on several existential matters. This volume reflects Brunstad's findings in his doctoral studies.

[21] Ibid., 28. Brunstad discusses the matter of secularisation in some detail and refers to several authors. He introduces Otto Krogseth's concept of the "dialectic theory of secularisation" which argues that even if religion is moved out of society's institutions, there is a sacralisation of individuals, and of cultural expressions. He notes that spiritual concepts like new age, Satanism, the occult, astrology and reincarnation became part of everyday language in the 1990s.

'desecularisation' and suggest spirituality—in multiple forms—will thrive in post-Christendom'.[22]

These observations carry significant messages for the Christian Church. If the Church wants to connect to people who want to be spiritual, it perhaps needs to emphasise the spiritual elements of its message more strongly. Aspects that could be lifted up would, for example, be the practice, use and power of prayer and meditation; understanding and living in contact with the Holy Spirit; the transcendent and near God; building values; building relationships; finding harmony, and living within creation with a holistic approach to the environment. These elements are biblical and still very relevant to the spiritual person. With the strong inheritance of spirituality from Christ, the Scriptures and the history of the Church, the Christian fellowship is a spiritual entity where people find resources for their own quest. The Adventist Church may need to consider developing in this direction.

So far it seems that the Danes, on an individual basis, have not become less spiritual—rather the opposite. Still, there has been a change in their belief systems; more people now think independently and tend to make up their own religion instead of accepting the guidance provided by the Church. Religion seems to have become individualised and privatised. This trend appears to connect with the secularisation of society as a whole, where religion is being moved into the realm of the family, private life and the individual. Pål Botvar defines the secularisation process in this way: 'The common way to define secularisation today is the process where religion and church lose their influence over spheres of society other than the purely religious. Secularisation can be understood as a form of narrowing of the legitimate place for religion'.[23] Bruce states that secularisation

---

[22] Stuart Murray, *Church after Christendom* (Milton Keynes: Paternoster Press, 2004), p. 148.

[23] Gustafsson, *Folkkyrkor Och Religiös Pluralism*, p. 74. This book is a report on the research programme *RAMP (Religious and Moral Pluralism)*, which is a European research project in twelve countries.

'maintains no more than that religion ceases to be significant in the working of the social system'.[24]

There are several reasons why Danish society has become more secularised. One factor seems to be the movement of people from rural areas to an urban setting. Pål Botvar reflects on this issue:

> Research on religious phenomena often emphasise that religion has its basis in the local community and in the social relationships we find there. Traditional, rural society was saturated by religion. In pre-modern homogenous culture it was difficult to distinguish between the religious and the secular. . . . Urbanisation leads to secularisation. By moving to the cities and by industrialisation one was moved away from nature and the natural processes of the life cycle. On top of that there was the pluralism of the cities. A third element is related to religious traditions—that in order to be sustained they have to find support in the social community of the individual. . . . Within the sociology of religion, the connection to a local community has been viewed as an important factor in relation to traditional religious belief and practice. In modern society this function is taken over by less stable and less formal social structures like family, neighbours and friends. [translation mine][25]

This observation has significance for the topic of this study—the discussion of the importance of relationships, networks and small groups in maintaining faith, in evangelism and discipleship. There are strong indications that it is the small, close community that keeps faith and religious practice "alive" in a person's life. Botvar continues: 'Changing one's dwelling environment contributes to

---

[24] Bruce, *God Is Dead*, p. 41. Quoting Wilson, Bruce also states that 'religion is not eliminated by the process of secularisation.' This is what is seen in the Danish population. Religion is moved to the private sphere of life. Bruce is the Chair of the deptartment of sociology at the Aberdeen University.
[25] Gustafsson, *Folkkyrkor Och Religiös Pluralism*, pp. 84–86.

removing the individual from the social structure which makes the religious concepts credible. Individuals, who used to practice their religion, can be pacified in a new living environment without the same plausible structure offered by religion' [translation mine].[26] Social and geographical mobility disconnect people from church and community.

Some argue that the process of secularisation also is connected to the change in people's educational levels and levels of welfare. There seems to be a relationship between secularism and financial independence. Sociologist Peter Ester presents this as a main hypothesis in his study in Norway: "The more economically advanced a country is, the more progress both secularisation and individualisation will have made, at least in Western democracies."[27] As Peter Ester reflects on the *EVS*, he notes,

> Those who grew up at a time when Norway was still a relatively poor industrial country harbour different values than those who grew to maturity when the country was developing into an oil-producing welfare society . . . the children of the 50s and later were able to pursue higher education, postpone marriage and children to have a career, and rely on the help of a strong public sector if needed.[28]

The idea that economic prosperity leads to secularisation, is questioned by Davie in *Europe: The Exceptional Case*. She notes that other parts of the world that have seen economic growth have not experienced the same process of secularisation. She refers to North America and South Korea where 'the economic indicators are some of the highest in the world, yet the religious indices are equally

---

[26] Ibid., p. 87.
[27] Peter Ester, *The Individualizing Society* (Tilburg: Tilburg University Press, 1994), p. 41. In this volume Ester reports on the *EVS* conducted in 1981 and 1990.
[28] Ibid., p. 295.

impressive'.[29] Ester also argues that the secularisation process is related to the 'growing influence of rationalism, individualism and consumerism'.[30]

Many political decisions contribute to move religion out of public life.[31] It is clear that public life has changed and that religion is being moved to a "side track" in Danish society. Also from Ester:

> Owing to this last development [the differentiation of social structures into autonomous sectors], religion and church have been privatised . . . religious and moral values, imposed by churches in the past, have become largely a matter of personal options. . . . The image of God as a personal God weakened as dependency disappeared and impersonal mechanisms replaced personal relations; the natural sciences fostered the idea of God more likely being a force than a "Person," if they did not destroy the belief in God altogether.[32]

One factor that illustrates the change in the place of religion in society is the space given to Christian faith in the Danish public schools. There has been a movement from instruction in Christian faith to "objective" descriptions of world religions in which Christianity is one of many. There has also been a movement from a position where Christian faith was presented as truth to a situation where all religions are presented as equally valid alternatives. The teaching of religious studies has acquired an information-based rather than a faith-based approach.[33]

---

[29] Davie, *Europe*, 141. Davie's comments are from 2002. Some evidence suggests that the US is going in the same secularised direction as Europe.

[30] Ester, *The Individualizing Society*, p. 39.

[31] It can be difficult to define whether political action is the response to the changes already taking place in a population – or whether they are leading that change.

[32] Ester, *The Individualizing Society*, p. 40.

[33] Peter B. Andersen, ed., *Religion, Skole Og Kulturel Integration i Danmark Og Sverige* [*Religion, School and Cultural Integration in Denmark and Sweden*] (Copenhagen: Museum Tusculanum, 2006), p. 16. This volume gives a

People's relationship to the Church has changed. Since more than 80 percent of the population are members of the National Lutheran Church through infant baptism, and less than 2 percent are members of other Christian denominations, some features of the Danish population's relationship to the main National Church are worth noting here. Four factors that illustrate this changing relationship are mentioned in the following paragraphs. The first clear indication of a change is that Church attendance is low and is continuing to decline. Church attendance is under 3 percent in Denmark, one of the lowest figures in Europe, on par with Belgium.[34]

A second factor in people's relationship to the Church is membership. The following table shows the membership in the National Church as a percentage of the total population.

Table 2.1. Membership in the National Church 1980-2011, in %	
1980	93.8
1990	89.3
2000	85.1
2011	80.4

Source: "Dansk Statistics," quoted in *Fremtidens Danske Religionsmodel*, p. 312

The change in membership is not only the result of people resigning from membership of the Church, but also a consequence of changing patterns in the population. The large inflow of immigrants to Denmark has brought people here who have other traditions and belong to other (sometimes national) Christian churches or to different religions altogether.[35] As a possible scenario for the future,

---

detailed description in the developments in policies for the subject of religion in the public school system.

[34] Ester, *The Individualizing Society*, p. 43.

[35] Christoffersen et al., *Fremtidens Danske Religionsmodel*, p. 313.
Christoffersen notes that many of the families from these backgrounds have many more children than Danes and therefore the population outside the National Church membership is growing faster than the traditional Danish population.

it can be noted that one prognosis indicates that less than 50 percent of the population in Copenhagen will be members of the National Church by 2020.[36]

An interesting nuance in the statistics on attendance is that although participation in regular Sunday worship is falling, there is an increased attendance at the time of festivals such as Christmas. Over a period of almost thirty years (1981 to 2008), people who said they seldom went to church went down from 70 to 59 percent. During the same period the percentage of people who said they went to church often went down from 13 to 10 percent. Those figures can seem contradictory. The answer seems to lie in the number of people attending church during the festivals. That percentage rose from 17 to 31 for the celebration of Christmas.[37] This can be interpreted to mean that people are using the church services to suit their own needs and family traditions. There is little conscious adherence to Christian doctrine, but the message of the Church at the festivals can be part of the individualised religion in each visitor.[38] This fits the overall picture of an individualistic approach to religious belief.

A third factor is the population's low adherence to Christian dogma—in spite of a seemingly stable level of faith. Even many churchgoers question the basic doctrines of the Church. This is particularly true of the members of the National Church. Members of other denominations, who also tend to be churchgoers, have a stronger adherence to the doctrines of their churches.[39] There is a close relationship between participation in Christian worship and the degree to which there is consent to the Church doctrines.[40] *The Danish*

---

[36] Lars Kolind, *Vidensamfundet* [*A Society Built on Knowledge*], 1 (Copenhagen: Gyldendal, 2001), p. 142. This stipulation is to some degree related to immigration of people with other religions.

[37] Christoffersen et al., *Fremtidens Danske Religionsmodel*, 314. Reporting on the findings of *EVS*.

[38] Ibid., p. 315.

[39] Gustafsson, *Folkkyrkor Och Religiös Pluralism*, p. 79.

[40] Ibid., p. 90; Bruce, *God Is Dead*, p. 73. Bruce also concludes that, 'There is a strong connection between churchgoing and holding Christian beliefs',

Pluralism Project concludes that 'only a small minority of members [of the National Church] attend ordinary church services regularly or express a traditional Christian belief. A majority are religiously alienated 'cultural Christians' who use the Church for religious festivals and transition rites'.[41] Even if most Danes are abandoning traditional Christian beliefs, they do not seem to be less spiritual. Ester comments:

> In spite of the fact that there has been a weakening of the dogmatic beliefs, the study [EVS] does not indicate that there is a general weakening of religious conviction. The numbers who state that they do not believe in any form of deity, god or spiritual power, have not increased. Religious belief does not seem to disappear, but it is becoming less and less dogmatic. . . . A lower participation in the services of the Church indicates that there is a privatisation of religion.[42]

Bjarne Hastrup, secular historian, makes this observation about the place of the National Church in society:

> The Danes distinguish themselves by the strikingly weak role religion has in the value patterns of the population. The paradox is that the state Church, with 84% of the population as members in 2002, is on the one hand an almost supreme religious institution in Danish Society but on the other hand the state Church has no significant influence on the other public institutions such as the public school system. Church attendance is steadily falling and relatively few Danes accept the State Church's answers on moral questions or family issues, but, however, still accept the Church's guidance on spiritual matters. Even if there is in Denmark, as in most of Europe, a faith in a

---

referring to research done by R. Gill (1999).

[41] Lars Ahlin et al., 'Religious Diversity and Pluralism: Empirical Data and Theoretical Reflection from the Danish Pluralism Project', *Journal of Contemporary Religion,* 27:3 (October 2012), 407.

[42] Gustafsson, *Folkkyrkor Och Religiös Pluralism*, p. 81.

god or a spiritual power, that does not express itself in any significant religious worship or practice. Quite the opposite [is true]. The Danes seem to be less religious than Europeans in general. [translation mine][43]

A fourth factor is the population's relationship to the main Christian written authority, the Bible. A study from Sweden was conducted by Anders Sjöborg in a doctoral research project at Uppsala University in 2006.[44] His study has a title saturated with meaning, *The Bible on My Own Terms*. It analyses Swedish people's relationship to the Bible in 1984 and in 2000 (when a new Bible translation was introduced in Sweden). Sjöborg found that Bible reading remained approximately the same; almost 10 percent of the population read the Bible with some regularity. Fewer people see the Bible as having a literal message (the numbers falling from 11.5 percent in 1984 to 7.1 percent in 2000) and fewer people believe that the Bible is inspired by God (43.7 percent in 1984, falling to 35.7 percent in 2000).[45]

Living in a secularised society has consequences for the individual. Botvar points out the difference:

> On an institutional level the privatisation of religion involves a situation where religion is transferred from public to private institutions. The public and collective framework around the individual's religious life crumbles, and other social systems, primarily the family, take over the role of maintaining the credibility of the religious world view. Within this perspective religion is not necessarily weakened by the modernisation, but it becomes detached from the official religious model and changes character—becomes less conventional. On an individual level a privatisation of religion happens in the individual

---

[43] Bjarne Hastrup, *Verdens Danmark* [*Denmark in the World*] (Copenhagen: Multivers, 2006), pp. 298–299.
[44] Anders Sjöborg, *Bibeln På Mina Egna Villkor* [*The Bible on My Terms*], Dissertation (Uppsala: Uppsala University Library, 2006).
[45] Sjöborg, *Bibeln På Mina Egna Villkor*, pp. 66–72.

consciousness. The individual will perceive and interpret himself and the world around him [as] independent of a religious frame of reference.[46]

The interviews with young people in Brunstad's research indicate that their relationship to the Christian faith is very much linked to their relationships to Christian individuals. He writes: 'The messengers, those who have been the intermediaries and representatives of the Christian message to the informants [interviewees], have played a crucial role when it comes to trust or distrust in the message [my translation]'.[47]

For the person who lives in a society where there is no reference to the Christian God and who has no connection to the Church, it usually requires another person to introduce him or her to Christian spiritual matters and to faith. It is in a relationship of trust that the secular mind can be opened to Christian faith.[48] George Hunter, in his classic book *How to Reach Secular People*, affirms this in his section on Strategies for Reaching Secular People: 'Secular people can be reached better by credible Christians in their kinship and friendship networks than by Christian strangers. . . . Churches who coach their people to reach the un-churched secular people in their social networks of relatives, friends, neighbours, and colleagues will find more of them receptive than the Church would guess'.[49] Hunter advocates setting up forums for dialogue and places to meet "credible Christians." The initial contact with—and reflection on—Christian faith happens best in a smaller social context – with a friend and in a small group.[50]

---

[46] Gustafsson, *Folkkyrkor Och Religiös Pluralism*, p. 75.
[47] Brunstad, *Ungdom Og Livstolkning*, p. 157.
[48] Lee Strobel, *Inside the Mind of Unchurched Harry & Mary: How to Reach Friends and Family who Avoid God and the Church* (Grand Rapids, MI: Zondervan, 1993). This volume describes this process. On pages 25-30 the author shows how a personal relationship started a journey of learning and reflection for his wife and himself.
[49] George G Hunter, *How to Reach Secular People* (Nashville, TN: Abingdon Press, 1992), p. 65.
[50] Ibid., pp. 57–60.

In his volume *Everlasting gospel—Ever-changing World*, Jon Paulien outlines some of the characteristics of the secular society and the secular individual. Like others he notes that even if organised religion seems to be in decline, spirituality is alive.[51] In his suggestions as to how the Church needs to move forward, his first point is, 'from public to relational evangelism'.[52] The emphasis is that spirituality is easier, more naturally and more convincingly shared by individuals who connect in an informal way, than by the religious establishment, which in many people's eyes, is suspect.

Although both Hunter and Paulien write from a North American perspective, their observations are clearly applicable in a Danish context; they correspond with the conclusions of Nordic research. This emphasis on relational or "friendship" evangelism has been on many Adventist pastors' lips over the years, but not much of that is happening. This might be a lack of understanding in leadership on how to move an organisation from seeing a vision to actually implementing that vision and establishing practices that make it happen. Another reason why not more is happening in relational evangelism, might be fear, laziness or the simple fact that people do not know many outside of church circles. Yet another reason might be the male dominance in church as men often tend to think more technocratic about their task and initiate programme-based evangelism. Maybe more women in leadership would help the church think more relational and less programme based and propositional. The evidence states that most people are open to genuine spiritual individuals who do not promote a system or an organisation, but have a life to share.

The change towards a more secular society has not had an immediate impact on the Adventist Church in Denmark. The Adventist Church has always been a small, minority movement in Danish society, with a rather anonymous existence over the last many decades. Because of

---

[51] Jon Paulien, *Everlasting gospel, Ever-Changing World: Introducing Jesus to a Skeptical Generation* (Nampa, ID: Pacific, 2008), p. 62.
[52] Ibid., p. 123.

the "monopoly" of the National Church, other smaller independent churches have played marginal roles in public life. There are, however, some current changes that affect the Adventist denomination.

The general secularisation of society means that the population which the Adventist Church is trying to reach has a decreasing knowledge and understanding of Christian faith and biblical concepts. One such example is that Christianity is no longer taught in public schools in a confessional way, if at all. The Adventist Church must conduct its mission and evangelism in a population that is becoming decreasingly biblically literate. The general disinterest in organised religion is also a challenge to the Adventist Church, but it may have a positive side in that a dialogue will start with a clean sheet. The Church has new opportunities since people are open, curious and do not carry some of the prejudices and preconceived ideas of past generations. In light of the little progress Adventists made in their first hundred years in Denmark, the church might well welcome the new culture and use every opportunity to connect with a new mind-set.

In this section it has been noted that Denmark is an increasingly secular society. Even if a personal faith persists in a large portion of the population, religious practices are in decline. This can be seen in falling church attendance, less agreement with church doctrine and a lower level of respect for the Bible. The number of people who have a religious faith is slightly increasing, but that faith is often undefined and not necessarily related to traditional Christianity.

Pluralism and Individualism

Since the time when the Adventist Church came to the country, Denmark has become a more pluralistic society. Migration, education, travel and modern media have all exposed the population to a variety of cultural and religious ideas. Pluralism is the coexistence of several cultural or religious expressions and identities within one population. In religion, pluralism may refer not only to the variety of religions in a society but also to the interaction between such faiths.[53] Below a relationship between pluralism[54] and individualism, will be established. Individualism refers to the thinking that each individual has the right to experience freedom and self-realisation, that each person may pursue his or her own goals and desires and—furthermore—value independence and self-reliance.[55]

Pluralism on the religious scene in Denmark has been well documented by the Danish Pluralism Project[56] at Aarhus University. The Pluralism Project is an interdisciplinary research project between different humanities departments at the University. In a 2012 article in the *Journal of Contemporary Religion*,[57] members of the research team presented data on the diversity of religion in Danish Society. They conclude that there is diversity within the Christian movement and that this heterogeneity is increasing. The National Church used to have almost a "monopoly" on religion. At present just over 80

---

[53] *The Shorter Oxford Dictionary* defines pluralism as "The theory that the knowable world is made up of a plurality of interacting things." *The Shorter Oxford English Dictionary: On Historical Principles* (Oxford: Oxford University Press, 2002), p. 2253.

[54] Ahlin et al., 'Religious Diversity and Pluralism', 404. The researchers in the *Danish Pluralism Project* choose to use the word "diversity" to describe the Danish situation since there is relatively little interaction between the different religious groups. The term "pluralism" is left to describe 'something more than diversity, namely the perceptions of diversity and new patterns of interaction among religious groups.' In this study the term pluralism is used just to describe the diversity and multiplicity of different groups. Ibid., pp. 404–405, 412.

[55] The *Shorter Oxford Dictionary* supplies this definition of individualism: 'Self-centered feeling or contuct as a principle; a way of life in which an individual pursues his or her own ends or ideas; free and independent individual action or thought; egoism.' *The Shorter Oxford English Dictionary*, p. 1359.

[56] Marianne C. Qvortrup Fibiger, 'The Danish Pluralism Project', *Religion*, 39:2 (2009), 169–75. This research began in 2002 at Aarhus University. At first it was a study of religious groups and their adherence in the City of Aarhus, but the study has since expanded to cover the whole country of Denmark.

[57] Ahlin et al., 'Religious Diversity and Pluralism', 403-418.

percent of the population of 5.5 million are members.[58] There is an increasing diversity in the National Church itself, with congregations having partly independent structures and slightly different emphases in their theology and practice.[59]

The membership of the National Church is decreasing due to people leaving and to immigration, as noted above. The Roman Catholic Church is growing, mainly because of immigration, and has 38,000 members.[60] Several independent churches (including the Baptists, Methodists, Salvation Army and the Adventist Church) have a few thousand members each. The Pentecostal movement is small, compared to the situation in many other countries, with seven- to-eight thousand members in Denmark. Immigration has brought many new Christian churches and groups to Denmark over the last forty years.[61]

The significant immigration that has taken place in Denmark over the same period has also brought several new religions to the country. There are 220,000 Muslims, 28,000 Buddhists, 12,000 Hindus, 7000 Jews and some alternative religious expressions like Scientology, Theosophy and the practice of ancient Nordic religions.[62] It is estimated that 40,000 to 50,000 people are engaged in these expressions to some degree and 6000 to 8000 to a high degree. New age religion is harder to define in numbers because its adherents operate in a more fluid way, often through centres for alternative medicine and education on living a holistic life. 'It is estimated that a

---

[58] (Infant) baptism is the entrance to membership in the National Lutheran Church. Most people follow the tradition to baptise their children. People can withdraw from membership at any time.
[59] Andersen, *Religion, Skole og Kulturel Integration i Danmark Og Sverige*, p. 413. The report mentions a new interest among "spiritual seekers" in engaging in pilgrimage, Christian meditation and other spiritual practices. "Church planting" and other evangelical movements create "alternative congregations which are more or less related to the National Church."
[60] Ahlin et al., 'Religious Diversity and Pluralism', 407.
[61] Ibid., p. 407.
[62] Ibid., pp. 407–411.

quarter of the adult Danish population use alternative therapies every year'.[63] These recent changes have brought many alternatives in terms of faith and worldviews to the attention of the Danes. Religion has become a "smorgasbord" to choose from. The individual is left with a larger responsibility than ever before, along with the freedom to choose his or her own way.

In this plurality individualism seems to flourish. Individualism and pluralism seem to feed into each other. Strong individualism creates a more pluralistic society and a more pluralistic society encourages more individualism. Commenting on the relationship between pluralism and individualism, Johannes Adamsen states: 'It is impossible to generalise the trends in Danish society. The very word pluralism indicates plurality. You cannot describe one new culture or one new spirituality. There are multiple cultures and multiple spiritualities in today's Danish society. The basis for pluralism is individualism. The church is therefore facing a multiplicity of different changes.'[64]

Pluralism and individualism are challenges to religious organisations. Introducing the *Religious and Moral Pluralism*[65] (*RAMP*) research project, Gustafsson states that 'according to Riis, the available data now suggest that the people in the Nordic countries are prepared to view several religions as bearers of truth'.[66] Writing in another part of the same volume, Botvar comments that 'the modern,

---

[63] Ibid., p. 411.
[64] Viggo Mortensen (ed.), *Er Kristendommen Under Forvandling?* [*Is the Christian Faith Changing Its Shape?*] (Højbjerg: Forlaget Univers, 2005), 63. Steen Marqvard Rasmussen makes a similar point in the same volume, '*At tage pluralismen alvorligt* [*Taking Pluralism Seriously*]', 87.
[65] Wilhelmus Antonius Arts and Loek Halman, *European Values at the Turn of the Millennium* (Boston: Brill, 2004), p. 8: 'The Religious and Moral Pluralism Project . . . is the first project aiming at investigating empirically the issue of pluralism in the domains of religion and morality. It is rooted in the Beliefs in Government project which was supported by the European Science Foundation.'
[66] Gustafsson, *Folkkyrkor Och Religiös Pluralism*, 30. Gustafsson refers to Ole Riis' chapter "Pluralism in the Nordic Countries." This volume summarises the results of research done under the name of *Religious and Moral Pluralism* (*RAMP*).

specialised and pluralistic society has created a credibility crisis for religion'.[67]

For many, individualism is seen partly as the consequence of, and partly as the root of, many of the other circumstances discussed in this chapter. There were various factors in Danish history that opened the way for individualism. Many of these changes have been parallel to changes in several other European countries. Mortensen traces society's movement towards individualism back to Martin Luther and the Reformation: 'When Martin Luther put faithfulness to his own conscience above the laws of society and the Church, he introduced a new understanding of the individual, which later in Western cultural history became part of the thinking about individual human rights'.[68]

Broad social movements have been at work, too. In Denmark the supremacy and rule of the royal family was broken in the 1840s. This opened the way for democracy. The National Church's monopoly on religion collapsed at the same time. A new constitution was formed and signed in 1848. It guaranteed the freedom of faith and worship.[69] It is not possible to trace these trends in detail within the scope of this paper. However, it should be noted that in the aftermath of World War II, as Danish society prospered, the rights and independence of the individual grew stronger. Higher education, a strong government welfare program, better financial conditions, women moving into the workplace and gaining more independence gave the individual more independence in relation to his or her family, the local community and society in general. Ester notes, 'Dependence has disappeared as a condition of daily life', as he comments on the developments in democracy, welfare and strong personal, private space.[70] He also notes, 'The social structure has been differentiated into separate,

---

[67] Pål Ketil Botvar, '*Kristen tro i Norden* [Christian Faith in the Nordic Countries]', in *Folkkyrkor Och Religiös Pluralism*, ed. Gustafsson, 76.
[68] Mortensen, *Kristendommen under Forvandling*, p. 24.
[69] Ibid., p. 25.
[70] Ester, *The Individualizing Society*, p. 40.

autonomous sectors: family life, work, community life, political life and church activities'.[71]

A powerful description of the move towards individualism comes from the qualitative study carried out by Furseth from Norway. She interviewed in depth eight people who had grown up in each of three different periods of time, the 1930s to1940s, the 1950s to1960s and the 1980s to1990s, with particular interest in their relationships to faith and to a faith community. The answers given in the interviews illustrate the fundamental change that has occurred in Nordic societies. The title of her book is in itself very telling: *From Quest for Truth to Being Oneself.* This rather lengthy quote summarises very well some of Furseth's conclusions:

> Due to the expansion of the educational system and the growth of the welfare state, they [those who grew up in the 1950s and 1960s] were able to pursue higher education and their own careers, and thereby, plan their own lives. They became the generation that wanted to "find themselves." Rather than accepting the values and traditions that were given to them, they set out to dissect every accepted norm and explore and form new ones. Whereas previous generations thought in terms of duty and obligations, Jan, Bente and Lise [interviewees] could think in terms of "creating their own lives." . . . Whereas the older generation [growing up in the 1930s and 1940s] perceives the group to be an important source of identity and sense of self, Jan, Bente and Lise [growing up in the 1950s and 1960s] largely see the group as entities that threaten the self. These stories reveal a shift in emphasis from an orientation towards others to an orientation toward the self, particularly in the area of religion. . . . In contrast to the middle-aged generation that attempted to "find oneself," Marianne [growing up in the 80s] takes for granted there is an inner subjective self that has true authority. For her, "being oneself" is a

---

[71] Ibid., p. 40.

fundamental concept that organises most of her ideas and experiences. . . It is her subjective self that creates order in life. For Marianne, groups do not constitute a theme for conflict. If she no longer finds that a group fits her sense of self, she will simply leave it. For her, it is her subjective self that determines her religious world views, morality, and group membership.[72]

In a similar way, Erling Birkedal concludes from his qualitative research, that 'It is a widespread attitude that each individual must be allowed to believe in their own way, and not only give support to, or rejection of, a faith given or provided by others'.[73]

A fundamental shift in people's relationship to religion can therefore be summarised as follows: 'The new emphasis on self implies that the post-war generation and their children only adopt these [the Church's] traditions if they fit with their personal enhancement or extensions of their own selves.'[74] This is similar to the conclusions drawn from the *EVS* by Lüchau. He states that the Danes take elements from many different sources to make up their own faith and worldview. Most Danes stay as members of the National Church since they find that their individual approach to religion can include a relationship to the Church. Nevertheless, he concludes that 'The Church can say whatever it wants, but the Danes will primarily listen when what is said, fits into their own private religious positions'.[75] He continues: 'In other words, the individualisation has made the Danes into members of the National Church on their own terms'.[76]

---

[72] Inger Furseth, *From Quest for Truth to Being Oneself* (Frankfurt am Main: Peter Lang, 2006), pp. 297-298.

[73] Erling Birkedal, *Noen Ganger Tror Jeg På Gud, Men . . ?[Sometimes I Believe in God, but . . .?]* (Trondheim: Forlaget Tapir, 2001), p. 133. This is a qualitative doctoral study on young people in the Norwegian National Church. There are close parallels to the Danish context.

[74] Furseth, *From Quest for Truth*, p. 298.

[75] Christoffersen et al., *Fremtidens Danske Religionsmodel*, p. 315.

[76] Ibid., p. 316.

Individualism creates pressure both from inside and outside the Adventist Church organisation. People who have grown up in the Church are influenced by an individualistic society and feel less obligated to be loyal to the Church, its teachings and traditions. Potential members from outside can express their liking of certain aspects of the "Adventist message" and at the same time feel indifferent or negative towards other parts. They will not necessarily have a feeling of loyalty to an organisation. The change towards individualism seems to happen by default and the church cannot stop it. The question remains whether, and how, the church can do its mission in this new setting. The Adventist Church has traditionally been very strong on its own identity and the particulars of its message. The issue of how it can relate to the new individualistic mentality, deserve more attention.

Davie makes two interesting observations in relation to Western Europeans' relationship to the national churches in their countries. As seen above, she argues that these populations are more unchurched than secular. She claims that for many the presence of the church has importance, even if they are not regular visitors to church services. She notes that in times of crisis, people's need for the church tends to surface. They meet in churches to find fellowship, comfort and meaning. She refers to this phenomenon in relation to the tragic circumstances of the sinking of the Estonia, the death of Princess Diana and the 9/11 attack in New York.[77]

The other consideration Davie mentions is that Europeans tend to let others keep religion alive on their behalf. She introduces the concept of "vicarious religion" and states that, 'Significant numbers of Europeans are content to let both church and churchgoers enact a memory on their behalf . . . more than half aware that they might need to draw on the capital at crucial times in their individual or their collective lives'.[78] These concepts seem to dovetail with the general

---

[77] Davie, *Europe*, p. 19.
[78] Ibid., p. 19. A curiosity at this point is that over 80 percent of the Danish population are members of the national Church and are willing to pay the

trend that Danes want to keep their National Church even though they have a rather loose relationship to it.

Adamsen makes an interesting observation on individualism. He states that it is a sociological phenomenon. It is something that happens to a whole people group.

> But individualism is basically a misunderstanding. It mistakenly presupposes that each individual is the basis for their own feelings and thoughts, as if these were not formed, in a significant and crucial way, by the surrounding community. . . . In reality the whole issue of individualism is carried by a cultural change, and for this reason it can be analysed as a phenomenon. If this was not the case, each single person could be understood on their own terms, with no common traits [translation mine].[79]

Closely linked to individualism is the concept of authenticity. To be true to oneself and to be who one really is, is seen by Danes as a high, even supreme, value. Furseth comments on authenticity when she writes about the move towards individualism in a Nordic context. She both defines it and remarks on its importance for different age-groups:

> In the stories analysed here, the discourse on authenticity centres on individual consistency between ideals and behaviour. . . . The shift in emphasis from an orientation towards the social group to an orientation towards the self is also revealed in the discourse on authenticity. Whereas the older generation [growing up in 20s and 30s] discusses individual sincerity in the area of religion in relation to one or more communities, Jan, Bente, and Lise

---

approximately 1 percent "church tax," which is collected through the government tax scheme. Only by withdrawing their membership can the Danes be relieved of this tax obligation. The fact that people are willing to pay 1 percent of their earnings to the church, show that it has significance for them.

[79] Mortensen, *Er Kristendommen under Forvandling?* p. 63.

[growing up in the 1950s /1960s] relate these topics to the self. They operate with a notion that they have a unique, inner, authentic self where truth is to be found. . . . For Bente and Marianne [growing up in the 1980s/1990s], to be genuine is related to the idea of "being true to oneself.[80]

A former president of the Adventist Church in Denmark expressed this insight on individualism back in 2004:

The biblical message has not been changed, but the last decades have put before us a new phase in the history of the Church. As several generations in the past have passed on the "relay baton" of truth to new generations, we have now reached a time when many must rediscover the gospel and the Adventist message, not just as a "readymade package," but as a result of their own seeking and finding. [translation mine][81]

This statement had perspective and caught the spirit of the times. In this study one aim is to suggest ways to bring this kind of understanding from being an observation, to becoming accepted, established and integrated in the behaviours of the organisation. This is the process of incarnational ministry. The church lives in tension and creative space between Jesus and the Scriptures on one hand and current culture on the other. John Stott expressed it this way: 'The church provides the text, the world provides the context'.[82]

Individualism and pluralism should not be seen only as threats to the church. There are opportunities. Pluralism in itself makes most people open-minded and, often, interested in another opinion. People are not stigmatised for being Christians and belonging to a church today, as it was in the 1970s and 1980s. An atmosphere of curiosity

---

[80] Furseth, *From Quest for Truth to Being Oneself*, p. 299.
[81] Andreasen, Carl-David, 'Træk Fra Formandsrapporten (Excerpts from the President's Report)', Adventnyt, 96 7/8 (2004), 9.
[82] John Stott, *Christian Mission in the Modern World* (London: Falcon, 1975), p. 29.

is an opening for the gospel. The opportunities and possibilities that come to the church will be discussed in the conclusion.

Interestingly, the Adventist Church came into being because its pioneers were individualists who dared to stand out from the crowd and hold unorthodox opinions. Some of that spirit is still around. The question remains if the Adventist Church can handle individualists in its midst today. The study of changes in Danish culture and society will continue in the next chapter.

CHAPTER 3

Changes in Danish culture and society – II

This chapter continues the discussion on changes in the Danes' relationship to issues of faith, spirituality and to the Christian church. The emphasis of this chapter is on postmodernism and a new spirituality. This chapter is followed by a discussion of the Adventist Church in Denmark.

Postmodernism

Postmodernism is a loose term which describes a new way of thinking and a new mentality. This change has taken place over the last half-century in most of the Western world. There are many factors in this change of mind-set, and it goes far beyond the scope of this paper to try to describe all aspects of postmodernism, its roots and its characteristics.[1] In this short section some of the elements of

---

[1] There is a wealth of literature on postmodernism. Some books that give a fair overview of the phenomenon include: Hans Bertens, *The Idea of the Postmodern: A History* (London: Routledge, 1994) and Steven Connor, ed., *The Cambridge Companion to Postmodernism* (Cambridge: Cambridge University Press, 2004). Significant writing has also been done on how postmodern thinking affects and relates to the Christian Church. This includes: Jim Belcher, *Deep Church: A Third Way Beyond Emerging and Traditional* (Downers Grove, IL: InterVarsity Press, 2009); D.A. Carson, *Becoming Conversant with the Emerging Church: Understanding a Movement and Its Implications* (Grand Rapids, MI: Zondervan, 2009); Gibbs, and Bolger, *Emerging Churches;* Robert C. Greer, *Mapping Postmodernism: A Survey of Christian Options* (Downers Grove, IL: InterVarsity Press, 2003); Stuart Murray, *Post-Christendom: Church and Mission in a Strange New World* (Milton Keynes: Authentic Media, 2005), Reggie McNeal, *The Present*

61

postmodern thinking[2] which would be likely to affect the relationship between the postmodern person and the Adventist Church are mentioned.

The first element is related to epistemology: the way people perceive, construct and arrive at truth. In terms somewhat like a caricature, it can be said that the postmodern person no longer believes in the Truth (singular with capital T) but in truths (lower case and plural). This is related to elements of pluralism and individualism which are described above. As people with different worldviews and religions live side by side, it is accepted that people see things from different angles, and that what is true for one person might not be true for another.

Stanley Grenz discusses the view that postmodernism is a challenge to evangelical Christianity. He writes about how evangelical Christianity was formed in and by the thinking of the time when it emerged, the Enlightenment:

> Postmodernism has tossed aside objective truth, at least as it has classically been understood. Foucault, Derrida, and Rorty stand against what has for centuries been the reigning epistemological principle: the correspondence theory of truth (the belief that truth consists of the correspondence of propositions with the world "out there"). This rejection of the correspondence theory not only leads to a scepticism that undercuts the concept of objective truth in general; it also undermines Christian claims that our doctrinal formulations state objective truth.[3]

Future: Six Tough Questions for the Church (San Fransisco: Jossey Bass, 2003); and Pete Ward, *Liquid Church* (Peabody, MA: Hendrickson, 2002).

[2] Some will argue that the term is becoming redundant as the youngest generations can no longer be classified that way. Terms that are used to describe younger generations would be metamodernism, posthumanism, neomodernism and a new materialism. Even if there is new changes on the way, the characteristics of postmodern thinking is present in the general population.

[3] Stanley J. Grenz, *A Primer on Postmodernism* (Grand Rapids, MI: Eerdmans, 1996), p. 163.

Grenz continues: 'Postmodernism questions the Enlightenment assumption that knowledge is certain and that the criterion for certainty rests with our human rational capabilities'.[4]

Grenz' opinion is challenged by others. Bruce, who writes on the process of secularisation in the West, argues that the way postmodern philosophy is relativising truth and knowledge is exaggerated. He insists that Western society still has faith in the rational: 'To put it simply, that we are no longer such enthusiastic cheerleaders for science, technology, social planning and economic growth as the Victorians does not mean that all ways of viewing the world have become equally attractive or plausible'.[5]

There are also different views as to how a postmodern epistemology relates to Christian thinking. In *Who's Afraid of Postmodernism* James K. Smith reflects on some of these issues. He goes beyond the superficial understanding some Christian writers seem to have about various postmodern philosophers. With the subheading 'Taking Derrida, Lyotard and Foucault to Church', Smith tries to go beyond well-known phrases to understand what these philosophers are saying.[6] He concludes that several postmodern positions may be closer to Christian pre-modern thinking than Christians tend to think.

He points out that postmodernism can be seen as a threat to a typically modern Christianity, but insists that there is more common ground than some critics[7] of postmodernism apparently believe. In relation to Jacques Derrida's famous statement, 'There is nothing outside the text', Smith tries to go beyond the immediate, superficial understanding. He opposes those Christians who interpret this statement to mean that there is no objectivity.[8] He states that

---
[4] Ibid., p. 165.
[5] Bruce, *God Is Dead*, pp. 232-233.
[6] James K. A Smith, *Who's Afraid of Postmodernism? Taking Derrida, Lyotard, and Foucault to Church* (Grand Rapids, MI: Baker Academic, 2006).
[7] See for example, Carson, *Becoming Conversant with the Emerging Church*, p. 43.
[8] Smith, *Who's Afraid of Postmodernism?*, p. 43.

Christians should not try to prove their faith in a modern way, but states that their witness will be more credible if they admit their basis for interpretation, are honest about their presuppositions and relate their convictions to faith, experience[9] and community.[10] He believes that a Christian response to postmodernism should be open and "up-front" about the nature of Christian thinking.

Christian apologetic teaching in a postmodern society should not try to prove the truthfulness of the Christian faith in a modernistic, scientific way but should rather admit that Christianity is built on faith, experience and the interpretation of the community. It should also emphasise that it works. The latter point is related to the postmodern definition of truth which also asks the questions "Does it work," "What is the outcome," and "Why is it important?" Smith's attempt to build a bridge between Christian and postmodern thinking is supported by other writers.[11]

What implications these philosophical and theological issues have for the Adventist Church should be looked at further. Individual members have taken initiatives in this direction.[12] These initiatives will not change things on their own. The Adventist Church in its totality has the challenge of expressing itself to a new generation. This is a leadership issue. Too often church leadership is about administering the status quo and keeping the peace. The mission-task given to the church, challenges leaders to face new times. Reaching out to the postmodern person will inevitably affect both the content of the message and the way it is presented.

---

[9] Ibid., pp.49-50.
[10] Ibid., pp.52, 57.
[11] See Caputo, *What Would Jesus Deconstruct?* and Downing, *How Postmodernism Serves (my) Faith*.
[12] One such attempt was done by Bruinsma in *Faith Step by Step*. Bruinsma makes an attempt to explain Adventist beliefs to a postmodern audience, and presents Adventist doctrines from a more existential point of view. A similar attempt has been made by Miroslav Pujic and Sarah K Asaftei in their book *Experiencing the Joy* (St. Albans: LIFEdevelopment Discipleship library, 2012).

A second important element in postmodern thinking is related to its understanding of epistemology, and that is the central place of interpretation and hermeneutics. All truth is seen as subject to interpretation. This allows for the idea that knowledge is subjective. D.A. Carson, in *Becoming Conversant with the Emerging Church*, discusses some of the basic propositions of postmodernism:

> Postmodernism accepts that there are methods, of course, but insists that there are many methods, all of which produce distinguishable results and none of which are more or less "true" than the results pursued by other methods.... Postmodernism therefore insists that objective knowledge is neither attainable nor desirable. At this point it finds itself in absolute opposition to modernism... postmodernism glories in the diversity of outcome.[13]

Grenz agrees: 'Postmodern scepticism, therefore, leaves us in a world characterised by a never-ending struggle among competing interpretations'.[14] Some consequences of this new pattern of thinking are an acceptance of diversity and an acceptance of relativism, the idea that things may be seen differently from different points of view. Third, knowledge is replaced by interpretation or construction. A fourth consequence is that there is no longer a single worldview. Fifth, there is an understanding of truth as being rooted in a social context. It is not hard to see that this challenges the way Adventist thought has been established, argued and presented.

There are authors who see this relationship in a different light. Crystal Downing, in *How Postmodernism Serves My Faith*, states that pre-modern and biblical Christian faith might differ from the modern Christian thinking that came out of the Enlightenment, and may instead include elements that are similar to postmodern thinking. She declares that Christian faith is related to experience and that the

---

[13] D. A. Carson, *Becoming Conversant with the Emerging Church*, p. 97.
[14] Grenz, *A Primer on Postmodernism*, p. 164.

Scriptures define truth as the person Jesus.[15] Truth is relational.[16] She goes on to say that Postmodernism does not support total relativism,[17] and that there is a balanced relativism which is healthy; a discussion is desirable.[18] She points out that truth is situated in a context[19] and that truth 'arises out of an interpretive community'.[20] This more relaxed position seems to be more balanced and truthful. Members of the Church need to learn to speak to others about their faith, recognising the presuppositions that also are a part of that faith. In this way Christians acknowledge they are making an interpretation of reality. Postmodernism invites everyone to experience openness[21] towards the other because it is aware of the limitations humans have in knowing all. This openness is also an invitation given to Christians.

A challenge to the Adventist Church that immediately rises to the surface is one of terminology. The Adventist Church tends to speak about its own set of beliefs in a less than humble language. This language has an internal history and interpretation, but can seem arrogant and at the same time naïve and simplistic, particularly when it includes the use of Adventist pioneers' expressions such as "the Truth," "the Present Truth," "the Last Warning Message" and "the Remnant." These terms were often combined with expressions that elevated the Adventist Church and condemned those who had different opinions.[22] The Danes are generally liberal and generous people who give space to all and recognise various positions as having

---

[15] Downing, *How Postmodernism Serves (My) Faith*, p. 177.
[16] Ibid., pp. 206–208.
[17] Ibid., p. 188.
[18] Ibid., pp. 198, 200.
[19] Ibid., p. 220.
[20] Ibid., p. 223.
[21] Ibid., p. 227.
[22] Words like "the remnant" and "God's last messengers" were used to describe the Adventist Church and terms like "Babylon" and "the fallen Churches" were used to describe other Christians. It is probably true that the jargon used back in the late-nineteenth century by Adventists was much more colourful and provoking than the terms and vocabulary common in the church's public statements today.

value. A rigid and too self-occupied approach clashes with the Danish soul.

To approach people in Western Europe with an apparent attitude of "knowing it all" and "having the complete answer" will not be attractive. People who are too certain are not credible. Making too strong statements appears naïve, simplistic and uneducated. All informed people know that knowledge is always increasing, even in religion, and that opinions have to change accordingly. Humility is strength in the proclamation of a position. In communication listening is as important as speaking. This is increasingly true in evangelism. A memory of the history of destructive disagreements and changes within the Adventist Church will help its members to practice this humility.

A third feature of postmodernism which follows the discussion on interpretation is subjectivity (as opposed to objectivity) and the significance of personal experience. If truth is relative, based on method of interpretation and the position held by the interpreter, each person has the right and responsibility to see things in his or her own way. This would be a popularised exaggeration of the true postmodern position as argued below, but is a position many Danes would take. At first glance this may seem to stand in contrast to Christian teachings, which to a large extent has been the communication of propositions. Grenz comments:

> Postmodern thinkers have given up the search for universal, ultimate truth because they are convinced that there is nothing more to find than a host of conflicting interpretations or an infinity of linguistically created worlds. . . . The abandonment of the belief in universal truth entails the loss of any final criterion by which to evaluate the various interpretations of reality that compete in the contemporary intellectual realm.[23]

---

[23] Grenz, *A Primer on Postmodernism*, p. 163.

Following this line of thought some will argue that if all is subject to interpretation then all truth is dependent on the person doing the interpreting. Each individual can thus make up their own truth and there is total relativity. This is not the position of postmodern philosophers. They do not take the argument to such extremes.

Downing discusses this issue. She quotes Richard Rorty (some people call him a postmodern relativist) to say that '"Relativism" is the view that every belief on a certain topic, or perhaps about any topic, is as good as any other. No one holds this view [no intellectually sophisticated thinker]. . . If there were any relativists, they would of course be easy to refute. One would merely use some version of the self-referential argument used by Socrates against Protagoras'.[24] Downing goes on to suggest that "pluralism" is a better term than "relativism" because pluralism indicates a plurality of understandings of the truth, whereas relativism tends to suggest that there is no truth. She quotes Rescher: 'Such a preferentialist position combines a pluralistic acknowledgement of distinct alternatives with recognition that a sensible individual's choice among them is not rationally indifferent, but rather constrained by the probative indication of the experience that provides both the evidential basis and the evaluative criteria for effecting a rational choice'.[25] Downing further states that there necessarily will be a pluralism of understanding also within Christianity. Human situatedness [the fact that all see reality from their own position] is a part of creation. She also refers to Smith who argues that, 'The truth, in creation, is plural', and also argues that since '"the New Testament writings are themselves interpretations of a person and an event we need to be open to differing interpretations of Scripture in our own day, trying to understand the situatedness of contemporary interpreters'.[26] In Downing's thinking truth is plural because it exists and is understood in relationships, communities and

---

[24] Downing, *How Postmodernism Serves (My) Faith*, pp. 190–191.
[25] Ibid., p. 200.
[26] Ibid., p. 201.

in an interdependent relation between the individual and reality.[27] This is in line with what John R. Franke writes in *Manifold Witness*, where he comments on human situatedness, and states:

> The expression of biblical and orthodox Christian faith is inherently and irreducibly pluralist. The diversity of Christian faith is not, as some approaches to church and theology might seem to suggest, a problem that needs to be overcome. Instead the diversity is part of the divine design and intention for the church as the image of God and the body of Christ in the World. Christian plurality is a good thing, not something that needs to be struggled against and overturned.[28]

The Adventist Church in Denmark is obliged to consider how it can better communicate in this type of intellectual environment. It should consider using different language about itself and its contribution. Understanding that the thinking of the church is coloured by its history, certain presuppositions and faith statements, may create a more humble approach to the presentation of a message. A part of witnessing is to recognise one's own presuppositions and hermeneutics (not only of the Bible, but of reality). Evangelism happens in a dialogue where all parties listen and there is an attempt to understand the platform from which another individual interprets reality differently. This is why Christian witness seems to become increasingly dependent on personal ministry.

The early Advent movement was influenced by the Enlightenment with its optimistic view of the attainment of knowledge and human ability to handle it. William Miller, not an Adventist but a forerunner of Adventism, sat in his home and studied the King James Version of the Bible with a concordance. He seems to have worked from the presupposition that everything in the Bible was one integrated system

---

[27] Ibid., pp. 205-206.
[28] John R Franke, *Manifold Witness - the Plurality of Truth* (Nashville, TN: Abingdon, 2009), pp. 7-8.

of ideas, and that as he studied it, he would see the whole structure of truth. Likewise, if all individuals were presented with the same facts, they would arrive at the same conclusions. The approach to the Bible inherited by the Adventist Church might be an obstacle in the conversation with postmodern people. A major question is whether Adventism can survive if it changes its approach to the Bible and the way it draws conclusions from it.

A fourth concept in postmodern thinking which challenges the Christian faith is the rejection of the "Grand Narrative" (metanarrative). The "–isms" which came into currency as a result of the thinking of the Enlightenment tended to be associated with a description of reality that was all-inclusive: worldview, ethics, understanding of history and the place of human beings in this reality all were included in a big story - the Grand Narrative.[29] The belief that human beings can achieve an integrated understanding of all aspects of reality is fading in the postmodern world. Simon Malpas comments on one of the intellectuals who have systematised postmodern thought: Jean-François Lyotard. Malpas describes how the belief in the metanarratives has disappeared:

> Alongside metanarratives that legitimate individual ideas and statements, Lyotard also introduces the concept of the grand narrative. Grand narratives are, for Lyotard, the governing principles of modernity. . . . Bringing together all of the different narrative and metanarrative forms of a particular culture, grand narratives produce systematic accounts of how the world works, how it develops over history, and the place of human beings within it. Put simply, grand narratives construct accounts of human society and progress. . . . The project of modernity, he [Lyotard] argues, has not been forsaken or forgotten, but destroyed, "liquidated."[30]

---

[29] Examples of grand narratives include the scientific metanarrative, the Marxist metanarrative and the Christian metanarrative.

[30] Simon Malpas, *The Postmodern* (Milton Park: Routledge, 2005), pp. 37-38.

In *Who's Afraid of Postmodernism*, Smith comments on Lyotard's critique of the metanarratives and tries to see if there is some element of truth in that position, from a Christian point of view. Smith recognises that the "metanarratives" are typical of the modern era. He argues that Lyotard is against the claims made by the metanarratives - the way and the why they are being told.[31] Lyotard thinks they are used to control and maintain power over people.[32]

The postmodern tend to focus on contradictory elements and on details rather than the total picture. Instead of looking for a metanarrative, the postmodern person relates to the "smaller stories" and finds it quite possible to hold on to seemingly contradictory ideas in light of his or her own or other people's experiences. The Adventist Church has a very clear profile in telling a grand narrative. It is called "the Great Controversy" and is a presentation of the biblical story from paradise to paradise restored, the fight between God and Satan; between good and evil. It is an explanation of how human beings form part of the battle between good and evil in the universe.[33] It may not be a matter of concern to the postmodern person that the Adventist Church has such an overarching story to tell. Its aspects are biblical and it provides a reference to an overall picture. The issue is rather the way the church presents this overarching story, and in what way it is sensitive to the fact that not every person's experience may fit into that story. In the same way, it must be able to look at biblical material, parts of reality, human experience and church life that do not seem to match the bigger picture.

---

[31] Smith, *Who's Afraid of Postmodernism?*, pp. 64–65, 68.
[32] Ibid., pp. 64-65, 68.
[33] Ellen Gould Harmon White, *The Great Controversy between Christ and Satan* (Mountain View, CA: Pacific Press, 1950). The Great Controversy theme is described in the book of the same name by Ellen G. White (one of the founders of the Adventist Church). She wrote a series of five books under the title *The Conflict of the Ages*, which is a kind of commentary on the Bible from beginning to end, with the perspective of a Grand Narrative.

Postmodern thinking also introduces opportunities for the church. People are not turned away by an unconventional opinion; diversity is accepted. As Paulien has pointed out people are searching for experience and community. Providing community in a smaller context, with honesty and authenticity, supplies an opportunity to witness, which needs include in the sharing of experience, spirituality and beliefs, included in its presuppositions.[34]

A change of a slightly different nature which is logical to introduce at this point is the issue of authority. Postmodernism, pluralism and individualism have brought about a different view of authority. Any organisation's right to state what is true or what one should believe is, at best, questioned. People question by what right an organisation can ask a person to comply with, and follow, certain ethical principles, lifestyles and value systems. Belonging is no longer seen as defined by a shared world view or grand narrative. In general people expect, and are comfortable in the presence of, differing opinions and views.

There is significant discussion in parts of the church about authority and, as a related issue, the role of leadership based on these changes in values. Gibbs and Bolger's *Emerging Churches*, describes this new phenomenon within Christianity and reflects on its connections to postmodernism.[35] Chapter 10 in their book discusses authority and leadership. Reflecting on modernity and how churches have been led, they state:

> Modern churches resemble this modern God. Their leadership is based on power, control, and submission to authority. For the church to resemble the Kingdom of God, current notions of church power must be drastically altered. The church needs to operate as a consensual process in which all have a say in influencing outcomes. The church should resemble

---
[34] Jon Paulien, *Everlasting gospel, Ever-Changing World: Introducing Jesus to a Skeptical Generation* (Nampa, ID: Pacific Press, 2008), pp. 121–133.
[35] Gibbs and Bolger, Emerging Churches, pp. 191–215.

God's beauty as it displays a peaceable community through the nonhierarchy of the priesthood of all believers.[36]

These authors go on to describe what postmodern thinking asks of church leadership. Their subheadings in chapter ten summarise their thinking:

> From stifling control to creative freedom
> From the vision of the leader to the vision of all
> From powerful group leaders to leaderless groups
> From leadership based on willingness to leadership based on gifting
> From leadership based on position to leadership based on passion
> From authority based on position to influence based on track record
> From closed leadership to open leadership
> From leaders setting the agenda to congregational agenda setting
> From exclusive decision-making to inclusive consensus-building.[37]

Of interest to this study is the statement 'Emerging churches form networks, not hierarchies'.[38] The emphasis is that each person has a contribution to give, and that wisdom emerges in a community which share their ideas and opinions. They write: 'Leaderless groups do not advocate no leaders, but simply that leadership be fluid, that all have a voice, that there be no named or appointed leader, and that leadership be flexible so that the right people lead the right things'.[39]

Tim Keel, in his book *Intuitive Leadership*, challenges traditional Christian leadership and tries to promote a different type of authority that suits "the emerging Church movement," and therefore also the

---

[36] Ibid., pp. 192–193.
[37] Ibid., pp. 194–204.
[38] Ibid., p. 195.
[39] Ibid., p. 198.

postmodern understanding of fellowship. He states that leadership in the medieval and modern churches is 'hardly distinguishable from other institutions within modernity that have enjoyed a long run of privilege and authority.'[40] Instead of a posture of authority Keel suggests that a leader should take on a 'posture of humility'.[41] Leadership and authority in the church come from Christ, as the head of the Church, to the whole body of the church. Leadership happens, is owned and delegated in the community.[42]

In Keel's argument leadership and authority in a hierarchical structure are no longer valued. It is the interactions of people in networks that correspond to postmodern values. A church community needs to work like a listening fellowship where all have a voice. In the words of Gibbs and Bolger, 'Leadership has shifted to a more facilitative role'.[43] This thinking on authority has significant implications for church life, and specifically its mission.

Leadership in the Danish Adventist Church has a challenge as it stands between a culture that operates on different values from those the World Church once employed. The Adventist Church has an interesting mix of democracy and hierarchical government. On the local church level there are strong democratic procedures for elections and constituency meetings. This pattern is largely the same when local churches gather in local conferences and have conference sessions with delegates from all local churches. Representatives from Conferences are delegates to the next level of administration: the unions. Again: representatives from unions form the delegates to the General Conference (GC) which is the head of the world church. From the local conference level and upwards it is administrators electing and representing administrators. Since the GC makes policies for the whole world church, these decisions will affect every

---

[40] Tim Keel, *Intuitive Leadership: Embracing a Paradigm of Narrative, Metaphor, and Chaos*. (Grand Rapids, MI: Baker Books, 2007), p. 116.

[41] Ibid., p. 230.

[42] Ibid., pp. 205-210, 220-221, 240.

[43] Gibbs and Bolger, *Emerging Churches*, p. 192.

local church. This system which has the intent of democracy, can turn into a tyranny of the majority. The Adventist Church is strongly hierarchical in that one local church does not have any real influence over decisions on policies and positions expected to be adhered to by all. This government style clashes with the values of the postmodern mind-set. In view of this, and an increasing diversity in the fast growing international church, the leadership in the Adventist Church might want to delegate more decisions to local fields and churches. The findings above on secularism, postmodernism and individualism will be further supplemented by a study of the emerging new spirituality.

New age and a new spirituality

The term new age is used as a label for a whole spectre of alternative and spiritual phenomena including established new religious movements, influences from eastern religions and contemporary popular spiritualities.[44] The new age movement has influenced and to some degree changed the mentality of the Danish people. However, few Danes are involved in this movement in a seriously committed way, such as to practice it as a religion.

Under the section on "individualism" in chapter 2, it was noted that Danish Christians in general, although remaining members of the National Church and remaining religious, increasingly tend to make up their own belief and value systems. These are often composed of elements from different religious traditions. The new age movement also seems to have influenced this change. *The Danish Pluralism Project* notes that one-quarter of adults in the Danish population use alternative therapies every year. This does not prove adherence to a particular philosophy or religious viewpoint, but 'it is a clear indication of their potential to disseminate alternative religiosity'.[45] The researchers in the project state:

---

[44] Steven Sutcliffe and Marion Bowman, *Beyond New Age: Exploring Alternative Spirituality* (Edinburgh: Edinburgh University Press, 2000), p. 1.
[45] Ahlin et al., 'Religious Diversity and Pluralism', 411.

We now live in a society that has largely left behind modernity with its fixed boundaries, its distinct and visible organisations, and thus also it's distinct and visible criteria for membership. For many people today, it is not a problem, and still less a conflict, to be affiliated with different available religions in different life situations. For example one might be a member of the National Church, with the possibility of using its rites of passage, not necessarily for religious reasons but more out of a need for orchestrating one's identity. At the same time, one can have a close connection with, even membership of, another religious organisation and meditate, for example, in a Hindu-influenced group.[46]

These conclusions are parallel to those drawn from research in Sweden.[47] Religion becomes a product in a marketplace where people can pick and choose. There is a mixing of religious thought. Marianne Fibiger refers to 'the many individuals who feel inspired by Asian religions when it comes to reincarnation, yoga, meditation, and personal development. These are examples of an individual patchwork religion and spirituality that we (*the Danish Pluralism Project*) believe can give an indication as to how religion is changing in Denmark'.[48] The dogmatic approach of organised religion is on the retreat and an individually defined spirituality is on the rise. Fibiger underlines this with her conclusion:

---

[46] Ibid., p. 414.
[47] Ahlin, *Pilgrim, Turist eller Flykting?* This volume reports on a quantitative study of 959 respondents to a survey which included questions relating to faith, religion and spirituality. Ahlin states that from the available material he concludes that, 'Only three percent can be classified as traditional Christian. That is the number of people who express a coherent traditional Christian set of dogmas and convictions... What most people do instead, is to freely combine components of beliefs from traditional and non-traditional faith systems, into a whole which fits their liking', p. 216. Ahlin likens the mixing of religious components to people 'constructing a self-identity,' p. 220.
[48] Marianne C. Qvortrup Fibiger, 'The Danish Pluralism Project', *Religion*, 39:2 (2009), 175.

The term religion in everyday conversation has somewhat ambiguous connotations to the ears of many Danes. Among these Danes, there was a trend to identify religion as an overwhelming and all-encompassing entity related to a specific dogmatic system to which they cannot relate. Instead they like to call themselves spiritual or spiritual seekers, both of which imply an acceptance of a form of transcendent or other-worldly reality without accepting any specified religious institution.[49]

The research done in the *EVS* clearly shows that the Danes' definition of God is moving in the direction of new age spirituality. This has been discussed above, but it is relevant here to note that the number who believed in a "personal God" fell from 27 percent in 1981 to 22 percent in 2008. On the other hand, those who believed in God as a "spiritual power" rose form 27 percent in 1981 to 35 percent in 2008.[50]

These observations from the Scandinavian countries are comparable to the findings of a qualitative study in focus groups in England.[51] People preferred to be seen as spiritual rather than religious. "Religious" was connected, in people's minds, with specific beliefs or with rigid opinions and seen as narrow-minded and immature. "Spiritual" was preferred as, for the respondents, it indicated openness and being informed. The researchers noted that most participants in the study who believed in something did not have any substance to discuss, as regards their beliefs, or language in which to explain what that "something" was,[52] but the researchers nevertheless noted that there was a remnant of Christianity in the group members' language

---

[49] Ibid., p. 174.
[50] Gundelach, *Smaa og store Forandringer*, p. 83.
[51] Kate Hunt, 'Understanding the Spirituality of People who do not go to Church', in *Predicting Religion: Christian, Secular, and Alternative Futures*, Davie Grace, Paul Heelas, and Linda Woodhead (eds.) (Aldershot: Ashgate, 2003), pp. 159-169.
[52] Davie, *Predicting Religion*, p. 163.

and understanding.⁵³ Kate Hunt summarises the observations from the focus groups with the statement, 'I'm not religious. . . I definitely believe in something'.⁵⁴

Two unrelated observations illustrate the change in spirituality in Denmark. The first concerns the development of the Theosophical Society (TS) and the second relates to the influence of television programmes on the topic of spirits. There has been a strong growth in the Theosophical Society in Denmark since 1980. This is documented by René Pedersen in 'The Second Golden Age of Theosophy in Denmark'.⁵⁵ Pedersen shows that the membership of the TS quadrupled from 1980 onwards, rising from approximately 300 to 1,200 members over the next twenty years. Pedersen sees one of the reasons for this growth in the fact that

> Key aspects of TS theology correlate very well with some fundamental tendencies in current society. Hence modern theosophy embraces the increasing individualisation that, particularly since the 1960s and 1970s, has pervaded Western societies. . . . I have also demonstrated that the expansion of the New Age or holistic milieu as such has been beneficial to the latter development and the rise of TS in Denmark – due to a widely held common set of dogmas and vocabulary.⁵⁶

The second point of interest is the influence of television programmes which focus on the spirit world. Merete D. Jakobsen has written on this phenomenon in 'Power of the Spirits: Spirituality in Denmark'.⁵⁷ Jakobsen reflects on the huge interest on the part of the Danish population in TV programmes featuring people who

---

[53] Ibid., p. 168.
[54] Ibid., p. 168
[55] Rene D. Pedersen, 'The Second Golden Age of Theosophy in Denmark: An Existential 'Template' for Late Modernity?,' *Aries*, 9 (2009), 233–62.
[56] Ibid., pp. 234–235.
[57] Merete D. Jakobsen, 'Power of the Spirits: Spirituality in Denmark', *Shaman: An International Journal for Shamanistic Research*, 14 (2006), 9–17.

claimed to interact with the spirit world. Two programmes were particularly prominent: "Power of the Spirits" and "Feeling for Murder."[58] Jakobsen notes that in the time period these programmes went on air (2000-2002, 2002-2004) there was an increased interest in workshops and fairs dealing with these issues: 'Now palmistry, clairvoyance, healing, etc. were dominating the scene'.[59] Jakobsen argues, with some hesitation, that the belief in a spiritual reality was filling a void because traditional Christian religion does not talk about the transcendent any more. She writes: 'It is interesting that while the spirits suddenly seem to appear frequently in ordinary households, at the same time the clergy in the state church in Denmark have become more and more reluctant to present Christianity as anything but a religion of compassion presently publicly struggling with the concept of God'.[60] She continues by suggesting a connection:

> There seems to be a very interesting dichotomy between a revival in a belief in the supernatural by the media and the Lutheran church simultaneously trying to explain that very world away; the miracles in the Gospels are described as just symbolic, the healing undertaken by Jesus only has the function to show him as "Son of Man," the evil spirits a metaphor for the dark side of human beings, etc. This demystification by the church might be understood as the reason for the renewed preparedness to accept the media's presentation of the intervention of spirits in everyday life.[61]

Jakobsen connects the willingness to believe in the spirits to an existential need to know there is something that transcends human life and something beyond the material world that is real. She is of the opinion that the National Church is failing to provide this perspective on life. She writes:

---

[58] Ibid., pp. 9–10.
[59] Ibid., p. 11.
[60] Jakobsen, 'Power of the Spirits', 12.
[61] Ibid., 12

> The rise in the media of an interest in the spirit world might be a direct product of this fear of meaninglessness. The existential angst has no object . . . . As God and the Holy Ghost in the Lutheran church are transformed into humanistic concepts such as love, compassion and peace, the television programs preserve a belief that ghosts are indeed real and interact with people's lives.[62]

These two rather disparate examples illustrate again the change in the spiritual climate in Denmark. They support the conclusions from the *EVS* and the *ESS* as described above.

A quantitative study among priests in the National Church shows that the priests have observed these same changes in Denmark. The results of the study are published in *Karma, Koran og Kirke* [*Carma, Koran and Church*].[63] When looking at the challenges facing the Church, 58 percent of the priests see secularisation as the biggest challenge to the Church.[64] Thirty-one percent consider the mix of religion [religionsblanding] to be the biggest challenge. That view does not refer to the presence of different religions in society, but to the mingling of different faiths in the thinking of individuals. People are open to different worldviews. Ninety percent of the priests in the National Church see this as a definite trend.[65]

The new vogue for mixing elements from different religious traditions, the openness to alternative world views and the focus on spirituality rather than religion also have an effect on those who call themselves Christian. Viggo Mortensen has described this in the following table taken from his book:

---

[62] Ibid., 13.
[63] Berit Schelde Christensen, Viggo Mortensen, and Lars Buch Viftrup, *Karma, Koran Og Kirke; Religiøs Mangfoldighed Som Folkekirkelig Udfordring.* (Højbjerg: Forlaget Univers, 2007).
[64] Ibid., p. 10.
[65] Ibid., p. 11.

Table 2.2. Viggo Mortensen's description of the Danes' change in understanding of God

Classic Christian Faith	New Spirituality
The distant God	God who lives within
We are sinners and need forgiveness	We are hurting and need healing
To do one's duty	To achieve self-realisation
God as Lord and King	God as friend and life giver
The proclamation of the Word	The mystery of the Eucharist
Understanding	Experience
Faith as believing truth	Faith as trust
The narrow gate	The wide embrace
Get to heaven	Live on earth
Philosophical truth	Psychological truth
("I mean that …")	("I feel that …")
Hierarchical authority	Authority based on experience
Strong borders – exclusivity	Soft borders – inclusiveness
Command	Enable
Obey	Guide, cooperate
Hierarchical relations	Mutual relationships

Source: Mortensen. *Kristendommen under forvandling [A Changing Christian Faith]*. 116.

The influence of new spirituality has significant similarities to the postmodern trends described earlier in this chapter. Both, in their own way, are part of the current zeitgeist.[66] Olav Hammer has found a link between the postmodern and new age. He compares the postmodern to the modern and notes that, in the same way, the new spirituality could be compared to classical Christian religion. He writes:

> If modernism stood for unity and integration, the postmodern condition is fragmentation, a kaleidoscope of disconnected parts. If modernism believes in

---

[66] "Zeitgeist" – *tidsånd* – is the "spirit of the time," the current thinking, values and attitudes.

scientific, rational reasoning, the postmodern also accommodates other expressions: play, feelings, experiments. Where the modern believes in a coherent personality, a whole "me," postmodern society is made up of people who are inconsistent, show different sides and without effort change from one view and style to the other. In these factors one can observe common values with the particular religiosity that thrives within the New Age. . . . The New Age does not build on arguments of reason or logically coherent reasoning, and it sees this fact as a strength rather than a weakness. New Age builds a poetic vision of the world which can be likened to a pre-scientific folk religion. But the style and the language are distinctly postmodern.[67]

Both new age and postmodernism challenge the modern mind-set and traditional Christianity.

Conclusions

Chapters 2 and 3 describe some of the significant changes in faith, values and spirituality which have taken place in the Danish population over recent decades. More factors could have been included; space does not allow for an analysis of all aspects of change. There are issues such as living standards, consumerism, the welfare state, educational opportunities, life expectancy and health issues, changes in family relationships, political changes, science and worldview and the introduction of the communication society, with the Internet and new social media, that all have an impact on individuals and society in general.

In spite of the general trends described in these chapters, on an individual level there is a plurality of opinions, styles, faiths and spiritualities. People have different interests and needs. It follows that

---

[67] Olav Hammer, *På Jagt Efter Helheden: New Age - En Ny Folketro* [*In Search of Wholeness*] (Aarhus: Clemenstrykkeriet, 1997), p. 270.

the Church should not conduct its evangelism and mission with only one type of person in mind.

Challenges seem to come to mind faster than opportunities as one thinks about the Adventist Church and its relationship to current Danish culture. There are, however, ways in which the Adventist Church can operate and do mission that will connect with the current zeitgeist. In chapter 6 two church plants will be studied as examples of communities that have been able to meet people's search for the spiritual. In their ministry the spiritual elements have been strong: worship, prayer, healing and community are key words.

CHAPTER 4

The Seventh-day Adventist church in Denmark

The Adventist Church has its roots in north-eastern North America. From there it spread to other parts of the American continent and beyond. The first Adventist missionaries went to Europe (Switzerland 1874), and the Scandinavian countries were among the first to be targeted (Denmark 1877). The beginnings of the Adventist Church in North America are well documented elsewhere.[1] It is, however, of interest for this chapter to summarise some of the thinking of the early Adventists and their approach to mission. The following areas are of particular interest to this paper: the context of change facing the church as it relates to the elements of invention, entrepreneurship and relevancy; the place of institutions in the ministry of the church;

---

[1] One historian that has written extensively on the history of the Adventist Church, is George R. Knight. See e.g. Knight, *William Miller and the Rise of Adventism* (Nampa, ID: Pacific Press, 2011), Knight, *A Brief History of Seventh-Day Adventists* (Hagesrstown, MD: Review & Herald, 2012) and Knight, *A Search for Identity: The Development of Seventh-Day Adventist Beliefs* (Hagerstown, MD: Review & Herald, 2000). Other works that describe Millerism and the early-Advent movement would be Sylvester Bliss, *Memoirs of William Miller* (Berrien Springs, MI: Andrews University Press, 2005), P. Gerard Damsteegt, *Foundations of the Seventh-Day Adventist Message and Mission* (Berrien Springs, MI: Andrews University Press, 1995), Leroy Edwin Froom, *Movement of Destiny* (Washington, DC: Review & Herald, 1971), Clyde E. Hewitt, *Midnight and Morning: An Account of the Adventist Awakening and the Founding of the Advent Christian Denomination, 1831-1860* (Charlotte, NC: Venture Books, 1983), C. Mervyn Maxwell, *Tell It to the World* (Boise, ID: Pacific Press, 1998), Arthur Whitefield Spalding, *Origin and History of Seventh-Day Adventists*, 4 Vols. (Washington DC: Review & Herald, 1961), and Richard W. Schwarz, *Light Bearers to the Remnant* (Mountain View, CA: Pacific Press, 1979).

methods of evangelism; and the number of workers assigned to different types of tasks in the organisation. These four issues will be discussed in two sections below. This chapter is not a historical overview of the Adventist Church in Denmark, but rather a reflection on some selected developments.

Beginnings in North America

The origins of the Adventist message lie in the US during the Second Great Awakening[2] and the Millerite movement.[3] William Miller (1782-1849)[4] was a farmer in Low Hampton, NY, and originally a deist. His experiences in the war with Britain challenged his position, and he came to believe in a more personal God.[5] This led him to start studying the Bible for himself. He believed that the Bible was self-explanatory and that unclear texts would find their explanations in other texts of the Bible. This optimism about the availability of knowledge and the sufficiency of the human mind was influenced by the Renaissance and the Enlightenment.[6] In Miller's time there was a strong optimism about man's ability to find facts, interpret them and have true knowledge of reality. It was thought

---

[2] Bruce Shelley and Adam Verner, *Church History in Plain Language* (Nashville, TN: Thomas Nelson, 1995), 385–386. See also Whitney R. Cross, *The Burned-over District: Social and Intellectual History of Enthusiastic Religion in Western New York, 1800-50* (Ithaca, NY: Cornell University Press, 1981).

[3] Schwarz, *Light Bearers to the Remnant*, pp. 37–51.

[4] Pedersen, *Syvende Dags Adventistkirken I Danmark*, p. 31.

[5] Knight, *William Miller and the Rise of Adventism*, pp. 24–27.

[6] Paulien, *Everlasting gospel, Ever-Changing World*. In chapter 4 Paulien discusses the influence of the Enlightenment on Christian and Adventist thinking. He compares this "modern" approach to knowledge to a "postmodern." See also Malco Bull and Keith Lockhart, *Seeking a Sanctuary: Seventh-day Adventism and the American Dream* (Bloomington, IN: Indiana University Press, 2006). Jim Belcher discusses the same issue from an evangelical point of view in *Deep Church*. He argues that the church is in captivity to Enlightenment rationalism in which the traditional church condones modern individualism, rationalism and pragmatism.

that if people had access to the same, and the right, information they would eventually come to the same, and right, conclusions. This optimism flowed over into religious contexts with the belief that if only the Bible was studied deeply and thoroughly, any student would come to the same explanation of all things.[7] Miller's approach was in the spirit of his times. He came with a creative and genuine attempt to understand his times with a method that seemed acceptable.

Miller's studies ignited a particular interest in Bible prophecies about the time of the end and the second coming of Jesus.[8] From his studies he concluded that Christ would return before the one-thousand years[9] described in Revelation (chapter 20), and that his coming would be soon. He experienced a divine calling to share this message,[10] so from the beginning of the 1830s, and with increased intensity, Miller proclaimed his prophetic understandings.[11] He predicted the Second Coming would happen in 1843. Later he changed the date to 1844, more precisely 22 October.[12] The 50,000[13] Millerites experienced "the Great Disappointment" when Jesus did not return. Most of them, and

Miller himself,[14] concluded that they had misinterpreted the prophecies and went on with their Christian lives. Some lost their religious faith. A third group kept seeking for better interpretations of key Bible passages used in the movement. This group of people

---

[7] Paulien, *Everlasting gospel, Ever-Changing World.*, pp. 16, 29, 30, 32.
[8] Knight, *A Brief History of Seventh-day Adventists*, pp. 14-15.
[9] Knight, *A Search For Identity*, 38. This position was contrary to the majority view at the time which taught a post-millennium return of Christ. Many thought that the world – and particularly the US – was moving into a thousand years of prosperity and peace; thus introducing the kingdom of God on earth.
[10] Knight, *William Miller and the Rise of Adventism*, pp. 35–39.
[11] C. Mervyn Maxwell, *Tell It to the World* (Boise, ID: Pacific Press, 1998), pp. 14-15.
[12] Knight, *A Brief History of Seventh-Day Adventists*, p. 21.
[13] Damsteegt, *Foundations of the Seventh-day Adventist Message and Mission*, p. 134.
[14] Sylvester Bliss, *Memoirs of William Miller* (Berrien Springs, MI: Andrews University Press, 2005), p. 6.

became the "movement" out of which the Adventist Church grew some twenty years later.[15]

Those who belonged to "the Little Flock"[16] continued to study the Scriptures with "modern" presupposition similar to those of Miller. A motive was to go beyond all traditions in Church history and find the original Christian beliefs and practices of New Testament times. They saw their efforts as being in line with the *Sola Scriptura* principle of the Reformation. There were five areas in particular where the early Advent Movement meant to find "new light" in the Bible.[17] An attempted coherent picture of reality—a metanarrative—was developed under the title *The Great Controversy*. A leading figure and a prophetic voice in the Advent movement, Ellen G. White, wrote extensively under this unifying theme.[18] The early Adventists called their new understandings "Present Truth." They saw themselves as a reform movement which was called to inform the rest of Christianity and the entire world about the "new truths" that they had discovered.[19]

Early Understanding of the Mission Task

The Adventist message spread westward from the north-east of the American continent. The idea of a mission task beyond North

---

[15] Damsteegt, *Foundations of the Seventh-Day Adventist Message and Mission*, pp. 100, 103–104.

[16] Leroy Edwin Froom, *Movement of Destiny* (Washington, DC: Review & Herald, 1971), p. 94.

[17] Damsteegt, *Foundations of the Seventh-Day Adventist Message and Mission*. This volume contains detailed information on the development of each of these doctrines. The five S's are the second coming of Jesus, sanctuary and judgment, Sabbath, state of the dead (and a holistic view of human beings) and the spirit of prophecy.

[18] The theme of "the Great Controversy" is described in the book of the same name by Ellen G. White. She wrote a series of five books under the title "The Conflict of the Ages" which is a kind of commentary on the Bible from beginning to end, with the perspective of a Grand Narrative (metanarrative). Ellen G. White, *The Great Controversy* (Mountain View, CA: Pacific Press, 1907).

[19] Ellen G. White, *Spirit of Prophecy*, Vol. 4 (Oakland, CA: Pacific Press, 1884), pp. 117–118.

America did not seem to occur to the pioneers.[20] Even if there were significant developments in the thinking on mission[21] in the Christian world,[22] early-Advent pioneers defined their own continent as their target. This can be illustrated by a question from A.H. Lewis, in 1859 in *The Review & Herald*, the main channel of information in the young movement. Lewis asked whether the Second Advent Movement should go beyond North America.[23] Uriah Smith, a leading figure in the movement, and resident editor at the time, gave a rather ambiguous answer.

He argued that the task of preaching the gospel to all nations could be achieved on the American continent because of immigration from all nations of the world. Smith added that foreign missions might be necessary in the future. As late as 1865 and 1867 Uriah Smith repeated his argument that bringing the message to all peoples could happen in the US. When the Adventist Church was established in 1863, a "Missionary Board" was organised as a part of its first constitution. In view of the meaning of the term "Missionary Board" in the world at that time[24] one would assume that its establishment included a vision for international work. In spite of this, the following decade saw little interest in foreign missions. A turning point was a key address at the General Conference Session in 1873 when James White presented a

---

[20] The information in this section is taken from a lecture by David Trim given for the Centre of Cultural and Religious Diversity, Newbold College of Higher Education, Binfield, UK, 18 March 2014: "Seventh-day Europeans? American and European Approaches to Mission in Europe 1880-1940." Trim is director of Archives and Statistics at the Seventh-day Adventist World Headquarters. The lecture is available on http://www.youtube.com/watch?v=272ma1g_9hQ (accessed 5 May 2014).

[21] Froom, *Movement of Destiny*, pp. 50–52.

[22] Some examples would be Adoniram Judson going to Burma as a missionary and Hudson Taylor to China. The British and American Mission societies were established and many mission boards throughout the Western world.

[23] A.H. Lewis, 'From Brother Lewis', *Advent Review and Sabbath Herald*, 13:11 (3 February 1959), 87.

[24] The many mission boards established in the world had a clear reference to international mission – particularly to the parts of the world where Christianity was not known.

strong appeal for the necessity to bring the Adventist message to all peoples and the entire world. This time the understanding was clearly to the nations outside the US.[25] In response to a plea from Sabbath keepers in Switzerland for support, the first Adventist missionary, J.N. Andrews, was sent there in 1874.

The Adventist missionaries who came to Europe brought an 'American religion'[26] with them.[27] Andrews had an authoritative leadership style, was self-dependent, worked hard and did not share his decisions with others. He was rebuked by Ellen White for working too much and not involving others.[28] Ludwig R. Conradi,[29] who took over the work in the German-speaking parts of Europe, had a more listening approach, and spoke about Adventism in 'European clothes'. He created links to people by showing that Adventism comes out of the Reformation and by finding roots for Adventist doctrines in European thinking. In his public preaching he tried to break down

---

[25] James White, 'The Conference Address', *Review & Herald*, 41:23 (May 1873), 180–181, 184.

[26] Pedersen, *Syvende Dags Adventistkirken I Danmark*, p. 22. Pedersen refers to the local newspaper, *Aalborg Stiftstidende* which wrote about Matteson representing the American Adventist Church.

[27] Trim, *Seventh-day Europeans?*

[28] Ellen G. White to J.N. Andrews, 29 March 1883. For more on Andrews and his attitudes and EGW's reproofs to him, see Harry Leonard, ed., *Andrews: Man and Mission*, (Berrien Springs, MI : Andrews University Press, 1985). Ellen White also rebuked the Swiss members for not listening enough to elder Andrews. In the following message she does seem to encourage the use of American models in Europe: "Elder Andrews is a conscientious servant of Jesus Christ, and your neglect of him was neglect of the Master who sent him. You might have instructed Elder A in some things, might have aided him with your sympathy, your love and cooperation; yet God did not send these men to be taught of you in regard to the best manner of managing His work. You should have been willing to be taught by Brother A, as one having a more mature experience in the cause of God." Ellen G. White, Manuscript Released No. 1230: 'Cooperation with God and Fellow Workers Necessary for Success in Fulfilling gospel Commission' (Washington, DC: Ellen G. White Estate, 23 January 1987), 323–324.

[29] For a description of Conradi's life and work see Daniel Heinz, *Ludwig Richard Conradi: Missionar Evangelist Und Organisator Der Siebenten-Tags-Adventisten in Europa* (Frankfurt: Peter Lang Publishing, 1998).

prejudice. Evangelism happened through smaller groups, literature evangelists and Bible workers. Conradi established schools in Basel, Hamburg and Friedensau (near Magdeburg) and in that way educated Europeans to carry on the Adventist mission.

This approach bore fruit and the Adventist Church grew faster in German-speaking Europe than in the US (reaching almost 25,000 members by 1914). The need for missionaries to listen to local culture was emphasised by Ellen White[30] and also stated in a speech at the 1897 General Conference Session by A.T. Jones.[31] To what extent the early Danish workers related to these issues, would need further study but the fact that Matteson, the first missionary to Denmark, had grown up there probably helped him to relate to local culture. The adjustments to new cultures demanded creativity and invention from the Adventist missionaries.

The Spirit of Invention and the Church Institutions

John G Matteson (1835-1896) had grown up in Tranekær (Denmark) before moving with his family to New Denmark, Wisconsin, in 1855.[32] It was in the USA that Matteson became a Christian and worked as a Baptist preacher for some years before becoming a member of the Adventist Church.[33] Matteson arrived back in Denmark, more specifically in the town of Vejle, in June 1877.[34] A man of multiple skills, he started preaching, teaching and visiting homes in several farming areas of western Denmark.

---

[30] Ellen G. White, *gospel Workers* (Washington, DC: Review & Herald, 1948), p. 462. See also *Letter 14* of 1887.
[31] A.T. Jones, 'Missionaries for God', *General Conference Bulletin*, 2 (First Quarter 1897), 14–20.
[32] Hans Jørgen Schantz, *I Troens Bakspejl* (Copenhagen: Dansk Bogforlag, 1998), p. 37.
[33] John Matteson, *Mattesons Liv Og Adventbevægelsens Begyndelse Blandt Skandinaverne* (College View, NE: International Publishing, 1908), pp. 54, 58, 82.
[34] Schantz, *I Troens Bakspejl*, p. 37.

Matteson came to a Christian country where the large majority of people shared basic Christian beliefs. Most people had an understanding of the Christian ideas of God, ethics, Jesus and his teachings, and a concept of salvation. Essentially the whole population belonged to the Lutheran State Church (hereafter: the National Church). In Matteson's view the Danes were neither spiritual nor religious and were not 'used to obedience'.[35] In his opinion both clergy and laity had a rather lax relationship to the Christian faith. In his preaching Matteson emphasised not only the gospel message, but also a radical lifestyle and discipleship. He presented the particulars of the Adventist faith. Major emphases were placed on the Adventist understanding of the Sabbath and the second coming of Christ. The presentation of these new doctrines quite often created quite a stir in the local communities. Priests or bishops would speak against this 'heresy'.[36] In his memoirs Matteson mentioned several incidents where mobs gathered outside the halls where he preached, and that he had to search for help from the local police. At other times it was the police who tried to stop him from preaching.[37] However, some Danes were open to new ideas and interested to hear Matteson's interpretations of the Scriptures. Others were captured by Matteson's appeal for a more radical lifestyle.

Matteson was soon joined by K. Brorson,[38] another American with Danish roots. They continued the preaching ministry together and soon they were supported in their work by some of the Danes who had accepted the Adventist message. The early Adventist evangelists used creative methods that were more aggressive than the more neutral invitation by the National Church with a "We are here, and you can come if you like" approach. They advertised in the newspapers with catchy topics and setting up posters with controversial statements or provoking questions. This created interest among the farming

---

[35] Matteson, *Mattesons Liv*, pp. 188–191.
[36] Pedersen, *Syvende Dags Adventistkirken I Danmark*, p. 19.
[37] Matteson, *Mattesons Liv.*, pp. 192–193, 199–200.
[38] Pedersen, *Syvende Dags Adventistkirken I Danmark*, p. 23.

communities. Matteson was a multitalented man. His challenging style was a new form of Christian preaching. It caught people's attention and even that of the local newspapers. A spirit of invention – and pragmatism – seem to have guided the early Danish Adventists. They did what worked in order to spread their message.

Institutions

The young movement in Denmark was innovative, and used methods that gave results. New members were seen as potential evangelists. The minutes from the national conference in 1886 state that there were 177 members and a further 116 Sabbath keepers nationwide. These 293 people were organised into small communities or churches.[39] Members were also enlisted in two societies: first, The Scandinavian Sabbath School Society [Den Skandinaviske Sabbatsskoleforening].[40] The society provided time for Bible study and sharing, and inspiration for mission. As several of the early Adventists in the US came out of the Methodist movement, Methodist ideas about small groups and societies were adopted by the Adventist Church. Sabbath School was conducted very much in the spirit of John Wesley's class meetings.[41]

The weekly gatherings, which were held before the worship service on Sabbath (Saturday) mornings, strengthened the early Adventists in their identity and their missionary zeal. Second, all members were

---

[39] *Forhandlingsprotokol 30/6-86 for Syvende Dags Adventisternes Konferens i Danmark. (Minutes from Negotiations of the Danish Conference of the Seventh-day Adventist Church)*, Handwritten document, 30 June 1886.
[40] Ibid.
[41] D. Michael Henderson, *A Model for Making Disciples: John Wesley's Class Meeting* (Napanee, IN: Evangel Publishing House, 2005), pp. 83 ff. Chapter 3 describes Wesley's five models for small groups: The society, the class meeting, the band, the select society and penitent bands. Sabbath School started as a (Wesleyan) class meeting with members of the group being accountable to each other and where there was Bible study, sharing, prayer and a ministry/mission emphasis. Over time this forum has changed more into what Wesley would call the Society: a class with a more cognitive emphasis.

encouraged to join The Scandinavian Literature and Mission Society [Traktat og Missionsforening].[42] Local meetings were held to train each member in spreading literature to neighbours and friends to introduce Christian faith and the Adventist perspective in particular.

Inspired by the Adventist Church in North America, the Church in Denmark established publishing, educational[43] and health[44] institutions. These were seen as missional both in the sense of improving people's lives and leading them to a commitment to Christ and "the Truth." The establishment of health institutions built on an ideological platform. The church acted out of social concerns, a motive of evangelisation and a holistic view of life. Adventists hold the belief that God's interest in human beings extended to all aspects of their lives and an emphasis on health stems from an understanding of the human body as 'the temple of the Holy Spirit' (1 Cor 3.16-17; 6.15-16). For this reason it was important to help people make choices about health issues and establish habits which would give them a superior quality of life.[45]

A similar ideology was behind the educational work. Education was not merely seen as passing on knowledge to a new generation

---

[42] *Forhandlingsprotokol 30/6-86.*

[43] Ellen G. White, *Education* (Mountain View, CA: Pacific Press, 1952). This volume outlines the Adventist philosophy of education.

[44] Ellen G. White, *The Ministry Of Healing* (Mountain View, CA: Pacific Press, 1942). This volume outlines the Christian principles behind the health work of the church.

[45] The Adventist Church recommends a healthy lifestyle. This is seen as a response to the idea that the human body is a temple for the Holy Spirit (1 Cor 6.15-16). Eight health principles that the church promotes are: 'Pure air, sunlight, abstemiousness, rest, exercise, proper diet, the use of water, trust in divine power—these are the true remedies.' These principles are taken from Ellen G. White, *Ministry of Healing*, p. 127. According to Seventh-day Adventist World Church Statistics the church is operating the following health institutions in 2013: Healthcare Ministry Hospitals and Sanitariums –173; Nursing Homes and Retirement Centers-132; Clinics and Dispensaries–216; Orphanages and Children's Homes–36; Airplanes and Medical Launches–10; Outpatient Visits–15,705,827. http://www.adventist.org/world-church/facts-and-figures/index.html (accessed 22 April, 2014).

but as helping each child to reach God's ideal and purpose for that individual. The school should lead the pupil in the development of the whole person in such a way that the child would grow up to have values, faith and a character that reflected Christ. The following words from Ellen White summarises this philosophy:

> True education means more than the pursual [sic] of a certain course of study. It means more than a preparation for the life that now is. It has to do with the whole being, and with the whole period of existence possible to man. It is the harmonious development of the physical, the mental, and the spiritual powers. It prepares the student for the joy of service in this world and for the higher joy of wider service in the world to come.[46]

The work of the school was seen as parallel to that of the church. Both had a redeeming purpose. Jesus would be the centre of education[47] as well as of the church.[48] The first local private church school was established in Jerslev as early as 1890[49] and the number of schools related to local Adventist churches grew to seven, which incidentally also is the number in 2014.

As for other institutions, a publishing house, *Dansk Bogforlag*, was set up in Copenhagen in 1906.[50] The first two health-ministry institutions were established near Frederikshavn in 1897 and north

---

[46] White, *Education*, p. 13.
[47] Ibid., p. 19.
[48] Seventh-day Adventists, 'Mission and Scope', http://education.gc.adventist.org/, *Education Department of Adventist Church*, February 2013, 1. This homepage gives some of the history of the development of Adventist educational work. This ministry has grown and is embraced in the Education Department which is responsible for the coordination, promotion, training, and quality of the global Seventh-day Adventist educational programme, which includes over 7800 schools, colleges and universities, with over 87,000 teachers and 1,680,000 students.
[49] Seventh-day Adventists, 'Skolens Historie' (The History of the School), http://www.xn--jf-lka.dk/index.php/skolen, *Østervrå-Jerslev Friskole*, n.d., 1 (accessed 2 November 2014).
[50] Pedersen, *Syvende Dags Adventistkirken I Danmark*, p. 105.

of Copenhagen in 1898.[51] Already in 1881, in the church's very first years, the Adventist Church began the publication of a *Health Magazine* (*Sundhedsbladet*).[52] The early Adventist missionary, John Matteson, started a Temperance Society in 1877.[53] For the relatively insignificant young movement with only a few hundred members, these were huge undertakings. The way the early Adventists exhibited strong vision and motivation, innovation and risk-taking is a challenge to the present established Church.

A very talented doctor, Carl Ottosen, became the pioneer of the church-related health work in Denmark,[54] establishing three sanatoriums, a school for cooks and physiotherapists, and a food factory that produced vegetarian alternatives to the heavy meat diet many Danes used. The main sanatorium, *Skodsborg*, and the food factory, *Den Sanitære Fødevarefabrik* (later *Nutana*), served the church and a wider market up until 1992.[55] It is of interest that by 1928, with total membership of 8183 in the three Scandinavian countries, there were 540 workers at the Adventist Church's sanatoriums and health institutions, and another 275 workers in private Adventist health institutions. The Church-owned institutions brought in an income of ten million kroner ($1.8 million) to the Church over a period of four years.[56]

---

[51] Ibid., pp. 85–86.
[52] Ibid., p. 82.
[53] Ibid., p. 82.
[54] Ottosen had visited the Adventist Sanatorium in Battle Creek, MI and learned from John Harvey Kellogg. Kellogg was a strong character and profile in the search for natural remedies to human illness and a promoter of a healthy lifestyle. Two volumes that describe his life and work are Richard Schwarz, *John Harvey Kellogg, MD* (Ann Arbor, MI: University of Michigan, 1965) and Brian C. Wilson, *Dr. John Harvey Kellogg and the Religion of Biologic Living* (Bloomington, IN: Indiana University Press, 2014).
[55] Pedersen, *Syvende Dags Adventistkirken I Danmark*, pp. 85–87.
[56] *Missionsefterretninger Fra Norge Og Danmark* [*Stories from the Mission Work in Denmark and Norway*] 9 (September 1928), 65.

Up until approximately 1930 the Adventist Church established its structures of operation and its institutions. After this time it continued in the same mode of operation. Memberships were growing as preachers led new people to the fellowship, and the running of churches and institutions was successful. Upuntil 1955 few significant changes took place.

The expanding Adventist Church found itself more resourceful than ever in the late-1950s. The membership was still growing, the average age of the members was relatively young, and the often hardworking and ambitious members were increasingly prosperous, due to strong growth in the post-war national economy. Many local fellowships wanted more convenient buildings in which to worship and operate their ministry. Obtaining better facilities would make church life easier and more attractive.

Among some there was a desire to make the Adventist Church more like a "church," and not only a "movement." They argued that if the Adventist Church had "proper" church buildings it would attract people interested in the Christian faith. Whatever the motivation, there was a strong building program in the church from 1955 to 1975. Of the forty-nine local fellowships nationwide, twenty-six built (or bought) new buildings during this period.[57] Members did not only give generously of their finances to construct and decorate new houses of worship, but also spent countless hours in volunteer work to keep costs down. For one or two years a local church congregation would do little more than worship together and labour to finish their building. Attention was drawn away from the mission of the church and its relationship to the local community.

Besides building and buying so many church properties, the membership raised money to build two retirement homes for the

---

[57] These building projects are recorded in the Danish Adventist Church paper *Adventnyt*. The facts have been summarised by Preben Jalving in ‚Menighedshuse opført I perioden 1955-1995' at HASDA.

elderly[58] and large investments went into providing several church schools with new buildings and better facilities.[59] Beyond that, two camp sites were bought and equipped.[60] In the twenty-year period from 1955 to 1975 the Adventist Church made vast investments in infrastructure and logistics. It is of interest to note how the church around this time (1962) moved into a plateau, and soon a decline, in its growth.[61] This seems to correspond to a life cycle for organisations which has been described by sociologists of religion.[62] The incredible investment in "hardware" had an impact on the mission of the church. It also figures as a paradox in light of the church's emphasis on the soon coming of Jesus. The relationship between the church's growing institutionalism and its membership growth is a topic of interest for further research and analysis.

Through the years the church has lost some of its institutions. The two major, and the last, were lost in the early-1990s. The church was

---

[58] Pedersen, *Syvende Dags Adventistkirken I Danmark*, 108. Solbakken (1973) in the western part of Denmark and Søndervang (1976) in the East.

[59] According to research by Birthe Bayer, 'Menighedsskoler opført I perioden 1955-1995' at the HASDA: Jerslev-Østervrå (1961), Two teaching buildings at Vejlefjordskolen (1965 and 1972), Torshavn (1966), Roskilde (1968), Ringsted (1969), Nærum (1974) and Århus (1975).

[60] Ibid. Kikhavn (1963) and Himmerlandsgården (1977).

[61] The Adventist Church had a membership of just over 4,000 in 1962. The present membership is approximately 2,500.

[62] Some authors who have observed a similar pattern in the development include: George Bullard, 'The Life Cycle and Stages of Congregational Development' (http://sed-efca.org/wp-content/uploads/2008/08/stages_of_church_life_bullard.pdf, June 2013); Alice Mann, *Can Our Church Live?: Redeveloping Congregations in Decline* (New York: Alban Institute, 2000); and Martin F. Saarinen, *The Life Cycle of a Congregation* (New York: Alban Institute, 1998). The pattern Saarinens describes, for example, is: birth, infancy, adolescence, prime, maturity, aristocracy, bureaucracy and death (p. 5). Research indicates that if a church does not experience a significant change, some new challenge or a significant new ministry every ten to fifteen years, that church will tend to reach a plateau in its growth and go into decline and extinction. There is the possibility for new growth at any time in that process from the plateau to decline, but it becomes increasingly difficult—and less and less likely—to revive, the further the organisation moves towards death.

forced to sell its health food company, Nutana, in view of impending bankruptcy, and the major health institution, *Skodsborg Sanatrium*, went bankrupt.[63] For many these were tragic events as the church lost its "flagships." In a modern thinking pattern the significance, success and strength of the church was seen in measurable entities such as numerical growth, institutions and buildings. Seeing the events from the angle of softer Christian values, others would argue that the Church may do better in evangelism and ministry without these large institutions. Some further reflection on the health institutions and their role will be done in chapter 6. The church schools have remained as contributions to the wider society.

Evangelism and the Disposal of the Workforce

The early leaders of the Adventist Church in America had put strong emphasis on literature. [64] It should be spread as 'leaves in the autumn'.[65] They realised that the written word would stay with people and teach them even after evangelists had left, and even carry their message beyond where they could send evangelists. [66] The early literature ministry in North America had an impact in the Scandinavian countries. Scandinavian immigrants to the US who had become members of the Adventist Church, had books and magazines translated into their own languages and saw it as a mission to send packages of literature to their relatives in Scandinavia.[67] It was

---

[63] These decisions and the meetings connected with them are described in some detail in the national Adventist Church Paper *Adventnyt*, 84 (March 1992), 10–11.

[64] Ellen G. White, *Testimonies for the Church*, Vol. 7 (Mountain View, CA: Pacific Press, 1948), 168–169. See also Ellen Gould Harmon White, *Christian Experience and Teaching of Ellen G. White* (Mountain View, CA: Pacific Press, 1940), pp. 225–226.

[65] Ellen G. White, *Ellen G White Manuscript Releases*, Vol. 19 (Silver Spring, MD: E G White Estate, 1990), p. 383.

[66] Ellen G. White, *The Colporteur Evangelist* (Mountain View, CA: Pacific Press, 1950), pp. 5–9.

[67] Kurt Faddersbøll, *Adventkirken Århus, Historie Og Begivenheder Gennem et Århundrede* (Århus: Private Publication, 1995), p. 14.

not uncommon for the early Adventist missionaries to find people who already adhered to the Adventist doctrines, as they travelled in Scandinavia.

As soon as there was a following for the Adventist message in Denmark, plans were made for a more organised publishing ministry. Already in 1881, when there were approximately 120 Sabbath keepers in Denmark, the literature ministry was emphasised in the first-ever board meeting for the young organisation: 'The distribution of literature is one of the most important methods for advancing the cause of Truth'.[68] The minutes also state, 'We have a printing press'.[69] The year after, 1882, the same Conference Board[70] mentions that literature evangelists were making thousands of house visits, selling books and magazines and leaving leaflets. This activity represented proactive and aggressive marketing. It was a new way of bringing a message to the people. Full use was made of the available media. It was combined with a personal interaction.

Emma Howell explained, as she later looked back at the early Adventist Church and its growth, that the three kinds of workers who particularly contributed to growth in

The early Adventist Church were pastors, literature evangelists and Bible workers.[71] These three, together with the 'influence of a Christian life', according to her, produced most conversions. Literature evangelists were self-employed but commissioned by the publishing house, whereas the pastors/evangelists and the Bible workers were employed by the church.

---

[68] *Forhandlingsprotokol 24/9-81 for Syvende Dags Adventisternes Konferens i Danmark. (Minutes from Negotiations of the Danish Conference of the Seventh-day Adventist Church)*, Handwritten document, 4 September 1881.
[69] Ibid.
[70] "Conference" is the term used in the Adventist Church for the fellowship and common administration of several local churches in an area.
[71] Emma E. Howell, *Den Store Adventbevegelsen* (Oslo: Skandinavisk Bogforlag, 1940), p. 115.

As the Adventist Church entered new areas, literature evangelists first did their house-to-house work. They sold books and magazines. They connected to people who were interested in spiritual matters and created some curiosity about the Adventist teachings, and came back to those homes over and over again. The main task was not to sell as many books as possible but to get to know people and introduce them to faith. After this work had been done, the pastor/evangelists would come to the area and conduct public meetings in several villages and towns at the same time. He (or she) would teach on general Christian topics and the specifics of the Adventist teachings.

While a preacher stayed in an area for many weeks teaching several times a week, a Bible worker was also there, assisting the pastor. Bible workers did extensive visitation among those who attended the meetings and their visits included care for the families, the giving of Bible studies, answering questions and sharing in prayer. Further study and clarification was done in relation to what was taught in the public meetings. The church had prepared particular *Bible Readings for the Home* for these visits.[72] The Bible workers' efforts would often continue for a longer time after the pastor had moved on to another field: 'Just as many make their decision in this time than who do it during the actual series of meetings'.[73]

Throughout the 1960s, 1970s and 1980s the main method of evangelism was still public meetings, small-scale or large-scale. Challenged by fading attendance, huge efforts were made to make meetings more appealing. There were series of public lectures on archaeology, natural sciences, history, Bible prophecy, health issues and other topics. A sense of frustration marked the church; methods that had created growth before brought very few results now. One of the later, and larger, public campaigns was held in Copenhagen in 1989 by an American evangelist, Mark Finley. A total of 2500 people attended seminars across the city on topics such as stress, the

---

[72] Ibid., p. 121.
[73] Ibid., p. 115.

Christian life, total health, the book of Daniel and more. Twenty pastors from the Scandinavian countries and a few lay people took part.[74] After the many seminars, a series of meetings was held at two venues in Copenhagen where seven-hundred people attended the first evening.[75] Some people joined the church fellowship through this large campaign, but the results were disappointing.[76] A few years later most of the new members were no longer attending church. In some way this major effort marked the end of an era of public evangelism as a principal strategy for reaching people in Denmark.

Around the beginning of the new millennium, some church plants were initiated.[77] The director for evangelism in the Trans-European Division, Peter Roennfeldt,[78] encouraged church planting in order

---

[74] Kenneth Jørgensen, ",Mod Høst 90 (Harvest 90)', *Adventnyt*, 81:3 (1989), 9.

[75] Rolf Kvinge, ,København for Kristus', *Adventnyt*, 81:4 (1989), 1.

[76] Reports from this large programme was almost absent from the church paper *Adventnyt* (AN). That tells its own story: relative to the initial high expectations there were few results to report. In AN 7/89, p. 11, there is a report from the board of the West Nordic Union. A short and vague reference to the meetings in Copenhagen is introduced by the words 'Public evangelism has become more difficult.' In AN 9/89 p. 6 there is an article on the results of "Harvest 90" internationally, but no mention of Copenhagen. In a short notice by Sven H. Jensen in AN 11/89, p. 26, there is an answer to the question, "What did the Copenhagen campaign cost?" The answer is 843,000 kroner ($160,000). There is no mention of any progress when it comes to the evangelistic result. Finally there is a report from the president of the church of the West Nordic union in AN 12/89 p. 3. There is a short thanks to God for what happened in Copenhagen, but no specific information as to how many people attended, made decisions for Christ or joined the church.

[77] In the late-1990s and the first few years of this millennium, four church plants were started: The Café Church in Copenhagen, Remix – a teenage ministry in Copenhagen, The Café Church in Aarhus and Face Out in Haslev. Later an English-speaking church was planted in Copenhagen.

[78] The Trans-European Division (TED) is a geographical entity of leadership and administration in Europe. It consists of sixteen unions of which Denmark is one. The Ministerial departmental leader for the TED at the time, Peter Roennfeldt, brought a strong emphasis on church planting into the TED through teaching, seminars and writing a manual for church planters: Peter Roennfeldt, *Planting Churches for Unchurched People*. (St. Albans, UK: Trans European Division, Ministerial Association, 2000). This emphasis was carried further by the next leader for this department in the

to attract a new generation and unchurched people. Church planting had not been tried in the Danish Adventist Church for a long time.[79] Some of these new churches were able to attract many unchurched visitors and attendance grew for a time.[80] They also created unrest in the established churches. Issues like worship style, music and choice of songs, the emphasis on the Holy Spirit with reference to healing and the speaking in tongues, created tensions. The young churches' faithfulness to the Adventist fellowship and its teachings, were questioned. Articles in the national church paper, *Adventnyt*, reveal this tension, and discussions and rumours certainly were more heated in less official contexts. There were critics[81] and defenders.[82] The national Adventist church magazine published articles on healing and the gift of tongues.[83] Central leadership emphasised the need for diversity and stated that new times require new methods.[84] The leader of one plant resigned from church employment for reasons of conviction, but mentioned the strong resistance from other members in a public statement.[85] Over time, the church wider membership

---

TED; Janos Kovaks-Biro. (Elected 2005.) See interview in *Adventnyt* , 5 (2006), 14.

[79] All churches have at one point been planted, but most churches have been planted a long way back in time, and growth in Denmark has mainly consisted of adding members to existing churches. The last church plant in the Danish Adventist Church before these was Lyngby Church, which was started more because of ideological differences than as an evangelistic project, in 1987.

[80] For an article on the Café Church in Copenhagen see *Adventnyt,* 96 (May 2004), 8, and for a presentation on REMIX see *Adventnyt,* 98 (January 2006), 7.

[81] One such article is Kurt Ravnkilde Nielsen Ravnkilde, ‚Knæfald for Ungdommen', *Adventnyt,* 96:12 (2004), 14.

[82] One example is Hans Stumpf, 'A Visit to an Adventist Café Church', *Adventnyt,* 97:6 (2005), 23.

[83] For samples of articles on these topics, see the national church paper *Adventnyt,* 5 (2004), 18; 6 (2004), 15; 4 (2005), 8-9; 6 (2005), 12.

[84] Carl-David Andreasen, 'The President's Report', *Adventnyt,* 96:7 (2004), 9–10. This article contains abstracts from the national leader's main speech and report to the General Session for the constituency in the Danish Adventist Church.

[85] Betina Wiik, 'Personal Statement', *Adventnyt,* 98:5 (2006), 23. In her statement Betina Wiik clearly states that – even though this was not the

came to accept the new plants, and in 2010 three churches were recognised at the constituency session and voted into full membership in the Danish Adventist Church.[86] The church plants have brought some growth but the success has been fading.[87]

A relatively new initiative that combines social work with Christian witness in a local community is Happy Hand in Copenhagen. That story will be covered in chapter 6, but it is of interest to note here that there is creativity in finding new platforms to share Christian witness. Most local traditional churches are looking for ways to lead new people to faith, but find themselves overwhelmed by the secular nature of society and repeated failures of evangelistic programmes they have initiated. The Adventist Church has, however, grown marginally after 2010 due to strong work among young church people and immigrants.

Workers

When the early Adventist Church's scattered communities grew in numbers, more resources were available for evangelism and mission. Finances were raised to pay full- and part-time workers. The minutes from the early years give some insight into the work of the paid staff. For example, in the minutes of 1882, there is a short mention of K. Brorson's report on his work. He often conducted four evangelistic meetings each week and spent the rest of his time visiting in local homes and spreading leaflets and magazines. In the space of a few months he baptised twelve people; nineteen were received as members of the Church.[88] Already in 1886, a very talented woman, Sine Renlev

---

reason for her resignation – there had been 'a lot of opposition' to the Café Church in Copenhagen where she had been the leader.

[86] Kenneth Birch, ‚Forvandling Og Fornyelse i Adventkirken', *Adventnyt*, 102:6 (2010), 11.

[87] A thorough study of the church plants, their development and their relationship to the "mother organisation" would be an important contribution to the Adventist Church's self-understanding and future mission endeavours.

[88] *Forhandlingsprotokol 30/5-80 for Syvende Dags Adventisternes Konferens i Danmark. (Minutes from Negotiations of the Danish Conference of the*

(1850-1899),[89] was employed and commissioned by the church as a Bible worker.[90] Bible workers were often skilled women who did extensive visitation in the homes. There were more women in church employment in the early years of Adventist history than today. They had a major role in bringing conviction and conversion. It is of particular interest to this study that the early work of the Adventist Church in Denmark depended heavily on the personal ministry that was done in homes. The significance of this will be discussed later.

That the early Adventists understood the importance of the personal element in evangelism can be seen from the employment statistics. There were more people doing personal work than preaching.[91]

Table 4.1. Church employees in Denmark, 1927

Workers	Numbers
Ordained pastors/ evangelists	9
Interns/ pastoral candidates	4
Bible workers	9
Administration/ Office workers	2
Literature evangelists	19

Source:

Forhandlingsprotokol 28/6-28 for Syvende Dags Adventisternes Danske Konferens.

> *Seventh-day Adventist Church)*, Handwritten document, First Minutes, 30 May 1880.

[89] 'Sine Renlev' (HASDA, 1999), 1. Sine Renlev was commissioned in 1886 as a Bible worker. This short article describes her significant contribution in evangelism. It also reminds the reader that women had central roles in the early Adventist Church.

[90] The term "Bible Worker" was used for assistants to the pastor/evangelist. The Bible workers would have some basic training in evangelism and in biblical understanding. Their tasks were to visit those who showed interest in the message, teach in the homes, answer questions, and care for the families.

[91] 'Planer for Evangelisme (Plans For Evangelism)', *Missionsefterretninger Fra Norge Og Danmark* [*Stories from the Mission Work in Denmark and Norway*] 10 (October 1928), 75. In this report from the leadership it is stated that the policy of the Church in sending out workers is to send "always a pastor and a Bible worker."

In 1927, the church grew by 225 new members. The number of members as of 31 December that year was 2622.[92] By comparison, the numbers for the whole Scandinavian Union,[93] including Denmark, Norway and Sweden, were as shown in the following table.

Table 4.2. Church employees in all of Scandinavia, 1928

Workers	Numbers
Ordained pastors/ evangelists	24
Interns/ pastoral candidates	10
Bible workers	26
Administration/ Office workers	6
Literature evangelists	150

Source:

Forhandlingsprotokol 28 June 1928 for Syvende Dags Adventisternes Danske Konferens.

For the whole Scandinavian Union the four years up to 1928 produced a net growth in the church of 1270 members in 160 local churches. Membership in 1928 was 8183.[94] A report from 1928 about the literature evangelists in Denmark shows that there were fifty-one active Literature Evangelists at that time (some part-time). In a year they did 33,338 hours of work, visiting homes, and sold items for 155,807 kroner.[95] This intensive visiting program in the homes, quite

---

[92] *Forhandlingsprotokol 28/6-28 for Syvende Dags Adventisternes Danske Konferens* [Minutes from Negotiations of the Danish Conference of the Seventh-day Adventist Church], *1928 – 1937.* (Handwritten minutes from conference sessions) (Copenhagen, 28 June 1928).

[93] The term "Union" is used in the Adventist Church to describe an organisational unit of several Conferences. A Conference is, as stated above, a common structure and administration for many local churches.

[94] Secretary, 'Report from the Scandinavian Union', *Missionsefterretninger Fra Norge Og Danmark.* [*Stories from the Mission Work in Denmark and Norway*] 65 (September 1928), 65.

[95] *Forhandlingsprotokol 4/6-29 for Syvende Dags Advenntisternes Danske Konferens (Minutes from Negotiations of the Danish Conference of the Seventh-day Adventist Church), 1928 – 1937.* Handwritten minutes from

unique for the Adventist Church, gave the church a strong impact in many local communities.

Later, in 1936, a report from the East Danish Conference[96] shows that there basically was the same balance between pastors and Bible Workers earlier.[97]

Table 4.3. Church employees in East Denmark, 1936

Workers	Numbers
Ordained pastors/ evangelists	8
Interns/ pastoral candidates	1
Bible workers	7 (4 women)

Source:
Rapport Fra Syvende Dags Adventisternes Øst-Danske Konferens, August 1936

There seems to have been a change in priorities, over time, when it came to the ministries of the church and what types of task the workforce in the Adventist Church was used for. For outreach, a Bible Correspondence School was established in 1947.[98] This organisation grew in the following decades and had two full-time, and one part-time employees. These workers answered two-hundred letters or more each week at the peak of the school's popularity in the late-1960s and early-1970s.[99] The running of several health institutions, operated both by the church and by private members, also tied up energy in institutional work. The nursing homes built in the 1970s absorbed

  negotiations, 4 June 1929. This figure represented about 8000 larger books, 6000 issues of a health magazine, 7000 issues of the evangelistic magazine, *Signs of the Times*, and besides these many shorter brochures and leaflets.
[96] The Danish church was split in two organisations – east and west in 1912.
[97] *Raport Fra Syvende Dags Adventisternes Øst-Danske Konferens (Minutes from Adventist East-Danish Conference)*, Handwritten document (Suomis vej 5, Copenhagen, August 1936).
[98] Pedersen, *Syvende Dags Adventistkirken I Danmark*, p. 107.
[99] Sven Hagen Jensen, ‚Historie - KS', 6 June 2013, 1. This information was provided by the current leader of the Correspondance School in an e-mail. There are no records in historical archives. Today the number of letters responded to is about 10 % of what it was in the 70s.

church-members into employment and voluntary engagement. The administration of the church grew too, after World War II. In tandem with the growth of the membership, but also in relation to funds available, the two conference offices in the eastern and western parts of Denmark expanded in sise. The following table shows a general shift in the organisation from "field workers" to administration and centralised functions.

Table 4.4. Church employees, 1927, 1973 and 2013

Workers	1927 all of Denmark	1973 West Denmark Conference	2013 all of Denmark (some part-time)
Ordained pastors/ evangelists	9	9	13.35
Interns/ pastoral candidates	4	2	3
Bible workers	9	0	0
Administrative/ Office workers	2	6	15.85
Literature evangelists	19	?	0

Source:

Forhandlingsprotokol 28/6-28 for Syvende Dags Adventisternes Danske Konferens, 'Organisation og Medarbejdere I Vestdansk Konferens, 31 December 1973', and Line Nielsen, 'Rejsen Sammen', http://adventist.dk/da/faellesskab/arsmode-generalforsamling-2013/sagspapir, *Generalforsamling 2013*, June 2013, p. 15.

The Literature Evangelist category no longer appears on the list. This is because the practice of selling door-to-door was prohibited in Denmark in 2004.[100] That made this house-to-house ministry impossible. The Bible Worker category has also disappeared. The new distribution of workers in the Adventist Church has significantly reduced personal contact in evangelism. This situation also redefines the role of the pastor in local churches. He or she alone carries the

---

[100] 'Lov Om Visse Forbrugeraftaler', https://www.retsinformation.dk/Forms/R0710. aspx?id=1843#K2, *(Laws on Trade Agreements)*, chapter 2, May 2013 (accessed 4 November 2014).

roles of pastor, evangelist and Bible worker. A more detailed analysis of the consequences of these changes for mission would be fruitful.

Closing remarks

The Adventist Church in Denmark has undergone great change, often externally generated. The stability of organisational structures, financial strength, functioning evangelism and a relatively homogeneous culture is gone.[101] Readjustment has been painful. Yet, in the middle of these changes, there are signs of progress. The latest reports from the union president and the union secretary documented numerical growth and envisioned a brighter outlook for the economy of the church.[102]

This chapter has presented a short overview of some aspects of the history of the Adventist Church in Denmark. The church has moved through periods of great change. From simple beginnings it grew to become more structured, settled, hierarchical and centralised. Over the years evangelism became more of a program than personal engagement, although some initiatives introduce a more personal and local approach as presented in chapter 6. As seen in chapters 2 and 3, Danish society has also changed dramatically. Faith, values, attitudes and relationships to religion have altered significantly. This scenario will serve as the background for the discussions on mission and evangelism in the following chapters.

---

[101] Two factors regarding the "homogenous culture" are the inflow of significant numbers of immigrants into the local churches. An English-speaking local church in Copenhagen has been established for mainly African and Asian worshippers. A second factor is that there have been many theological discussions in the church over the last decades and there is now a diversity of opinions on several issues in the church. It goes beyond the scope of this paper to discuss these matters further.

[102] Nielsen, 'Rejsen Sammen', 14. The vice president of the Danish Adventist Church reports that as of 31 December 2012 the church had 2506 members, ten members more than two years earlier. Although symbolic in sise, that was a positive message to a church that had seen decline for many years. More analysis of the last few years may emerge in later research.

PART TWO
THEOLOGICAL REFLECTION

CHAPTER 5

Theological reflection on the church and its mission

This study is concerned with the Adventist Church and its ministry in times of cultural change, and specifically the changes that have happened in Denmark over the last couple of decades. The following theological[1] reflection will not deal exhaustively with the church and its mission,[2] but rather focus on some selected issues. References to scholarly work will be used to direct the reflection. Two New Testament books which give input into this particular discussion have been chosen. The first is Acts of the Apostles, which is of interest with its record of the first years of church history including major changes in theology and missiology. Of particular interest is

---

[1] The term theology comes from the two Greek words *theos* and *logos: theos* meaning "God" and *logos* meaning "word" or "speech." Theology is then literally language about God: Richard Rice, *Reign of God: An Introduction to Christian Theology from a Seventh-day Adventist Perspective* (Berrien Springs, MI: Andrews University Press, 1997), p. 2; speaking or thinking about God; Fritz Guy, *Thinking Theologically: Adventist Christianity and the Interpretation of Faith* (Berrien Springs, MI: Andrews University Press, 1999), p. 4. To do theology is to seek to understand what God is like, what His will is and what He does. As Stanley Grenz and Roger Olson state: 'Theology is the study of God, His attributes, and His relationship with man and the Universe'. (Stanley J Grenz and Roger E Olson, *Who Needs Theology? An Invitation to the Study of God* (Downers Grove, IL: InterVarsity Press, 1996), p. 37.

[2] The words *mission* and *missionary* come from Latin words with the meaning of "send" and "one sent." The Bible usually employ the word *apostle* to describe one who is sent in a particular way; it is translated from the Greek word *apostolos* which means one who is sent as a representative or an ambassador.

the longer narrative of 9.32 to 15.35, which describes key events in the church's acceptance of gentile converts and a growing missionary endeavour to "the whole world," thus carrying particular insights for times of change. With reference to these dramatic stories, four issues will be discussed: Jesus and Mission, the Holy Spirit and Mission, the future and Mission and leadership and Mission.

The second biblical book selected for a somewhat shorter reflection is the epistle to the Ephesians, which includes Paul's most thorough teaching on the church.[3] Three issues will be discussed: The "in Christ" principle, the church and unity in the Spirit. There will, of course, be references to other parts of Scripture and other literature.

Reflection on Mission in Acts

Jesus and Mission

The biblical book of Acts is a continuation of the gospel according to Luke.[4] Both are written by and to the same person, Theophilus, and Acts make clear references to the material in Luke in its introduction (1.1). The story in Acts starts where Luke ends with Jesus giving his last words of comfort and challenge to the disciples.[5] Jesus' commissions and the promise of the Holy Spirit create further links between the two books (Luke 24.46-49; Acts 1.7-8).[6] Thus the

---

[3] John Stott, *The Message of Ephesians: God's New Society* (Leicester: InterVarsity Press, 1989), pp. 126–130.

[4] David J. Williams, *Acts - New International Biblical Commentary New Testament 5, Subsequent Edition* (Peabody, MA: Hendrickson, 2002), p. 19.

[5] The authorship of Luke and Acts is discussed in scholarly circles. The issue is not crucial for this study. The continuation is argued by Robert L. Gallagher and Paul Hertig, *Mission in Acts: Ancient Narratives in Contemporary Context* (Maryknoll, NY: Orbis Books, 2004), 4-6; and Williams, *Acts*, 2–5.

[6] In commenting in Acts 1.8 NIBC answers the question of how Jesus continued his work after his ascension. It was the power of the Spirit of Jesus that lead the apostles forward. We are reminded of the words of Jesus saying that those who would listen to the disciples would listen to him (Luke 10.16). They had now become like their teacher (Luke 6.40). So it was in Jesus's name healing and preaching was done. (Acts 3.6,16; 9.34; 16.7). Williams, p. 14.

story of the church is presented as a continuation of the story about Jesus. Christ is central to the book of Acts as he is presented as the initiator of the story, he is the content of the message of the story and the story unfolds under the guidance of his Spirit. Thus Acts is highly Christological.[7] The link between Luke and Acts also provides a continuum from the story of Jesus in his Jewish context to the gentile Christianity of later years,[8] and the open ending of the book points to an unknown future which will still take place under the continued leadership of the Spirit of Jesus.[9]

Jesus defines the content of mission of the church. Jesus claimed that his deeds and his message came from his heavenly Father[10] (e.g. John 8.16-29; 12.44-49; 13.20; 14.24). The mission of Jesus was to teach, proclaim and heal.[11] In Jesus's first sermon in his home town, Nazareth, he chose a passage from Isaiah to illustrate what his task was. It is recorded in Luke 4.18-19, and includes elements of proclamation, social justice, healing and restoration.[12] Jesus sent his disciples to the world with the words 'Peace be with you! As the Father has sent me, I am sending you' (John 20.21). The church is called to take the pattern for its mission from the example of Jesus.

---

[7] Gallagher and Hertig, *Mission in Acts*, p. 315.
[8] Williams, *Acts*, p. 14.
[9] Gallagher and Hertig, *Mission in Acts*, pp. 321–322.
[10] Jon L. Dybdahl, 'Missionary God - Missionary Church', in *Re-visioning Adventist Mission in Europe*, ed. Erich Walter Baumgartner (Berrien Springs, MI: Andrews University Press, 1998), p. 8.
[11] See the parallel verses Matt 4.23 and 9.35. These texts both state the same three elements of Jesus's ministry and narrate the stories of Jesus actually doing that in the chapters between.
[12] Luke's citation from Isaiah is somewhat creative, leaving out some parts of the main source, 61.1-2, and adding elements from 58.6. Thus Luke establishes Jesus as introducing the "year of the Lord" and gives him a clear Messianic mission. The emphasis on Jesus as healer and releaser corresponds with Luke's description of Jesus' ministry. For a more detailed discussion on Luke's rather "loose" citation of the prophet see Darrell L. Bock, *Proclamation from Prophecy and Pattern: Lucan Old Testament Christology* (Sheffield: Sheffield Academic Press, 1987), pp. 105–117 and Joel B. Green, *The Theology of the gospel of Luke* (Cambridge: Cambridge University Press, 1995), pp. 76–82.

That mission has its origin with God is an important truth to remember as churches sometimes can come to think that their mission is to promote their own message and institution. The church always has to come back to a humble position recognising that their task belongs to someone greater. In *Missional Church,* it emphasised this idea: 'We have come to see that mission is not merely an activity of the church. Rather, mission is the result of God's initiative, rooted in God's purposes to restore and heal creation'.[13] Jon Dybdahl puts it this way: 'Mission is the mother of the church, not the church's daughter'.[14]

In his Sermon on the Mount, Jesus said that his followers should be "salt" and "light" in the world (Matt 5.13-16). They will spread the understanding of, and the blessings of, the kingdom of God.[15] Reggie McNeal states this plainly in *Missional Renaissance*: 'The role of the

---

[13] Guder and Barrett, *Missional Church*, p. 4.
[14] Baumgartner, *Re-Visioning Adventist Mission in Europe*, p. 5.
[15] The leading theme of Jesus's teachings was "the Kingdom of God" (also expressed as "Kingdom of heaven"). His sermon on the mount (Matt 5-7) reflected on the principles of the Kingdom. Many of Jesus' parables related to the Kingdom (e.g. Matt 13). The coming of the Kingdom was a response to the promises of the OT about the introduction of God's rule in the world. Jesus inaugurated the Kingdom and demonstrated what it was all about. Arthur F Glasser and Charles Edward van Engen, *Announcing the Kingdom: The Story of God's Mission in the Bible* (Grand Rapids, MI: Baker Academic, 2003), pp. 183, 200. Jesus stated that the kingdom was near, in the lives of his followers and present in his own life (Matt 4.17; 12.28; Luke 17.21) and called his message the "gospel of the kingdom" (Matt 24:14). The kingdom and the church are not the same. The kingdom is where God rules (Luke 11.20). Raoul Dederen, *Handbook of Seventh-day Adventist Theology* (Hagerstown, MD: Review & Herald , 2000), p. 543. Jesus sent his disciples out to proclaim the kingdom, not the church (Matt 10:7). Jesus never spoke about his disciples as the Kingdom. Since the kingdom centers on Christ, the church relates to the kingdom in that those who follow Jesus can enter the kingdom (Mark 9.47; Matt 7.21; Luke 16.16). Jesus challenged his listeners to "seek first his [God's] kingdom and his righteousness" (Matt 6.33). 'It is clear from these references that the language is metaphorical and must be understood in the sense that man now has the opportunity to 'enter' a new way of life in which God's will becomes the norm.' Donald Guthrie, *New Testament Introduction* (Leicester: InterVarsity Press, 1981), p. 713.

church is simply this: to bless the world'.[16] He compares this to God's purpose to bless all nations through the seed of Abraham (Gen 12).

The church follows the example of Christ through acts of love, service, proclamation and witness to the Lordship of Christ. Charles van Engen, in *God's Missionary People,* identifies four key concepts that describe the church's role in the world: 'The missionary church emerges when its members increasingly participate in the church's being-in-the-world through *koinonia, kerygma, diakonia* and *martyria*'.[17] *Koinonia* refers to the fellowship of love that should exist among the followers of Christ; *Kerygma* refers to the proclamation of the lordship of Jesus Christ and the kingdom of God; *Diakonia* is the service and ministry the church does in the world to provide healing, reconciliation and justice; and *Martyria* is the witness of the church about God through words and actions. Just as Jesus saw himself as a servant (Matt 20.28; Mark 10.45), the church goes into the world in a spirit of servanthood; not with power or worldly authority. Jesus taught his followers that they should serve each other and the world as they spread the knowledge of the kingdom (Mark 9.35; 10.41-45). The church continues in the footsteps of Jesus, participating in the Mission of God as Jesus did. The practical ministries of the church grow out of its understanding of mission.

In light of the strong Christ-centered message of Acts, a church leader (or member) naturally asks him- or herself if their church lives up to that ideal. Somehow churches tend to turn into self-preserving entities as they age. Both local congregations and larger denominational structures tend to move towards an unhealthy self-interest. Rather than making Christ and his kingdom the focus of attention, concerns about membership numbers, the defence of one's own doctrinal correctness, finances, business involvement, educational

---

[16] Reggie McNeal, *Missional Renaissance: Changing the Scorecard for the Church* (San Francisco: Jossey-Bass, 2009), p. 46.

[17] Charles Edward van Engen, *God's Missionary People: Rethinking the Purpose of the Local Church* (Grand Rapids, MI: Baker Book House, 1991), p. 89.

institutions and even multi-million corporations can move the church towards a selfish agenda.[18] In a postmodern setting where most people are sceptical towards large institutions, whether spiritual or secular, the church will need to constantly repent and be converted to have its priorities right. This generation has developed a nose particularly sensitive to the smell of institutionalism and hypocrisy.

The Holy Spirit and Mission

After the ascension of Jesus, the first significant event in Acts is the outpouring of the Spirit at Pentecost. Peter explains the phenomenon referring to the promise through the prophet Joel that at the end of time the Spirit will be 'poured out on all people' (Acts 2.17-21; Joel 2.28-32).[19] As noted by Michael Green, there have been many outpourings of the Spirit in the history of Israel, but at various times and in a selective capacity. As a fulfilment of the prophetic promise a new era of the Spirit was announced at Pentecost.[20]

In a similar way Guder emphasises the centrality of the Holy Spirit in Acts: 'The church owes its origin, its destiny, its structure, its ongoing life, its ministry - in short, its mission—to the divine Spirit of life, truth and holiness. At Pentecost, with the outpouring of the Holy Spirit, promise becomes actuality'.[21] The chapters following tell stories of supernatural intervention. Dreams, prophecies, hearing the voice of God, healings, raising the dead and exorcisms were all parts of a story where God was leading the infant church to achieve its mission task. As the Christian movement expanded from a Jewish context in Judea on to Samaria and to the whole gentile world,

---

[18] John Muddiman, *The Epistle to the Ephesians: A Commentary* (London: Continuum, 2001), p. 48.

[19] All Scripture quoted is from The New International Version, unless otherwise noted. Biblica Inc., *The Holy Bible, The New International Version* (Grand Rapids, MI: Zondervan, 1973).

[20] Michael Green, *30 Years That Changed the World: A Fresh Look at the Book of Acts* (Leicester: InterVarsity Press, 2002), pp. 248–249.

[21] Guder, *Missional Church*, p. 145.Mich.

extraordinary events confirmed its divine origin.[22] In Acts, the Holy Spirit has a corporate function[23] and leads the movement forward in unison. Eddie Gibbs points out that the outpouring of the Spirit at Pentecost was according to Jesus' promise of power to bear witness:

> The greatest evidence of that experience [baptism of the Holy Spirit] is that individuals are empowered to witness for Christ whose Spirit they have received (1.8; 4.31). Therefore, the Pentecost phenomena must be interpreted according to Luke's intention, which is distinctively missiological. For Luke, the baptism in the Holy Spirit is not primarily concerned with salvation, or even a "second work of grace," but with the essential empowerment of the church for its witness throughout the world. The disciples were not waiting upon the Lord primarily for their personal renewal, but rather to receive corporate empowerment for their mission.[24]

The establishment was challenged. The progression in mission and theology was not guided by the decisions of a committee or the advice of theologians in Jerusalem, but came as the result of divine intervention. The story of Peter and Cornelius, which is given seventy-four verses and is retold three times in part (Acts chapters 10, 11, 15), emphasises this truth: dreams and divine intervention opened the way for new thinking and practice. The space given to this story indicates that it is one of the most important stories in Acts. By the outpouring of the Spirit on new gentile believers, God made the

---

[22] Gene L. Green discusses the supernatural phenomena in Acts in 'Finding the Will of God; Historical and Modern Perspectives' in Gallagher and Hertig, *Mission in Acts*, pp. 210–216. She recognises that supernatural phenomena were common in pegan religions, too, but is of the opinion that Christian manifestations were of a different character.

[23] Michael Green notes that whereas in Acts the Holy Spirit has a corporate role and function, he is more of a personal Spirit in the epistles; like in Ephesians which will be discussed below. Green, *30 Years That Changed the World*, p. 260.

[24] Eddie Gibbs, 'The Launching of Mission; The Outpouring of the Spirit at Pentecost' in Gallagher and Hertig (eds.), *Mission in Acts*, pp. 20–21.

theological statement that they were as acceptable to Him as Jewish Christians.

Today's Adventist Church, and most other established churches, are challenged by this story. Rationalism, with its need to control circumstances and events, so easily takes over. Creativity and intuition are often set aside for the safe guidance of tradition and past experience. The story of Acts invites a spirituality that is open for the unexpected[25] and a God that will do what has not been done before. In its endeavour to reach the changing population in Denmark, the church must ask itself if it is living in a maintenance mode upholding traditions, or whether it is open for a Spirit-led leap to new understandings and practices.[26] A recent leader in the Adventist Church in Europe, Bertil Wiklander, makes the following comment on the story of Peter and Cornelius: 'God, the God of mission, the Holy Spirit, was leading out, and the church had to struggle in order to follow'.[27] The church today faces the same challenge.

The Spirit was not given for personal enjoyment. It was given for mission. Spiritual gifts are given to the community through individuals (1 Cor 12.7) so that the community can serve more and better. Whether a church is charismatic or not, it must remember that the blessings received are for sharing and not only for personal profit. True revival and reformation come through being part of God's mission in this world, not by introspection.

The Future and Mission

As the church in Denmark faces new and different times, it lives in the tension between the past and the future. Seeing God's leading in the past, and having a strong commitment to discovered truth, to change anything – the style of presentation, the message, or the

---

[25] Green, *30 Years That Changed the World*, p. 152.
[26] Ibid., pp. 9–10; pp. 192–194.
[27] Bertil Wiklander, 'A Vision for Mission renewal in Europe'," in Erich Walter Baumgartner (ed.) *Re-Visioning Adventist Mission in Europe* (Berrien Springs, MI: Andrews University Press, 1998), p. 257.

methods for ministry and mission – might be seen by some as a compromise. There are encouraging understandings coming from Acts. Particularly the episodes in 9.32 through 15.35, which shows divine leadership that brought the church into an unknown future. Van Engen's comments: 'Are all these events simply coincidences? Clearly Luke was seeking to describe a well-orchestrated, carefully-designed chain of events that could only be the work of God'.[28]

The path towards the new was not uncomplicated as leadership, the centre for influence, the makeup of the membership, and the geographical point of gravity changed in the church. These movements will be discussed further in the next chapter, but several scholars describe these changes under the general heading of 'From Jerusalem to Antioch'[29] and divide Acts into two parts according to the same thinking.[30] Key leadership is moved from Peter and Jerusalem to Paul and Antioch. Peter is profiled as the key leader in the early chapters of Acts, particularly with his public speech on the day of Pentecost (chapter 2) but also through leadership, healing and traveling in consecutive chapters. After the crucial episode with the household of Cornelius (chapters 10 and 11) his role in Acts weakens and he disappears from the story after a short appearance in chapter 15. Paul, on the other hand, takes over as the key figure and trendsetter some years after his conversion (chapter 9) as he and Barnabas are sent out as missionaries from Antioch (12.25-13.3) – not Jerusalem.[31] From

---

[28] Charles E Van Engen. 'Peter's Conversion: A Culinary Disaster Launches the Gentile Mission', in Gallagher and Hertig (eds.), *Mission in Acts*, p. 138.

[29] Ray S. Anderson, *An Emergent Theology for Emerging Churches* (Downers Grove, IL: InterVarsity Press, 2006), pp. 4-5.

[30] Hertig and Gallagher give Acts a two-part structure. Peter (chapters 1-12) Paul (13-28). The first part was represented by Jerusalem, the second by Antioch. Gallagher and Hertig, *Mission in Acts*, p. 10.

[31] In 'The Forth Pentecost' Pettis argues pp. 250-251 that the centre of power changed from Jerusalem to Antioch. He argues the same issue through what he calls "the four Pentecosts." 1. Jerusalem with the elders – the 11 apostles (Acts 2), 2. Samaria (8.14-17) with Peter and John, 3. Caesarea (10.44-48) Peter alone, and 4. Ephesos (18.18-26) Paul. No longer is one of the 12 needed.

this time the centre for expansion of the movement, and for guiding and encouraging the gentile mission, is Antioch. Jerusalem and Peter's role fade.[32]

The adjustments to the gentile mission did not come through a carefully designed strategy document from the leadership, from the decisions of a committee or from theological reflection in an institution; they come through the intervention of the Spirit and as responses to events on the ground, the members and leaders taking pragmatic, bold and Spirit-led decisions in response to their situation. Thus the church acted more as an organism than an institution. In the words of Michael Green:

> Through the Spirit and mission the Kingdom is demonstrated to the world before the return of the King. The Spirit and the Church belong together, but it is noteworthy in Acts that the Spirit always takes the lead. The Church can only live by evangelising, and by following the paths that the Spirit indicates. It was not the church leaders who decided on an evangelistic campaign. It was an ex-Pharisee, converted through opposing them, who was the main agent in that outreach under the prompting and the power of the sovereign Spirit of God.[33]

The church may not be—and probably should not be—the same tomorrow as today or yesterday. The story of Acts shows that the Kingdom of God sometimes grows in an unexpected fashion. The Spirit moves an organic movement. Even the headquarters change: if not formally, then in practice. Decisions will have to be made where the action is. When set structures fail to recognise to meet new challenges, the Spirit leads people to make new moves. The apostles in Jerusalem probably could not learn much from the past? The new gentile mission was a completely new paradigm. Also for the church today, as people and circumstances change at an increasing speed,

---

[32] Green, *30 Years That Changed the World*, p. 194.
[33] Ibid., p. 254.

the past becomes less and less relevant, a thought which might be uncomfortable for both leaders and members. Experience is good, and there are lessons of the past to learn from, but a lot of experience cannot be transferred to an entirely new situation. Sometimes the church, its leaders and members, have to admit that that they all stand with blank sheets of paper. According to Acts, it is the Spirit who knows the future who can lead the church into an unknown future. Roger Greenway makes this encouraging conclusion from Acts: 'God is always ahead of us'.[34] Church leaders and members should not be afraid of some chaos, and uncertainty and confusion may not be the main enemies of the Christian community.

Cooperation with the Spirit demands openness, creativity and a sanctified intuition. These values are rare in established institutions. The church will, for example, have to decide whether it will take the risk and listen to younger people, new members and visitors who tend to understand the present times, and trust that they will be faithful to the calling of Jesus, and even the church, as they relate the message to a new time.

Leadership and Mission

Young movements and organisations are often driven by strong visions, high energy levels and a strong spirit of volunteerism and sacrifice; so also with the young church in Acts. Although there is no systematic presentation in the book about leadership and structure, reading between the lines gives the impression of a people movement where major responsibilities were shared according to spiritual gifts and practical necessity, and little attention was given to position. Formal structures seemed few and scarce, and tasks and responsibilities were distributed according to present needs. The hierarchical models which often characterise church organisations today, seemed non-existent except for the authority of the elders and apostles in Jerusalem

---

[34] Roger S. Greenway, 'Success in the City: Paul's Urban Mission Strategy', in Gallagher and Hertig, (eds) *Mission in Acts*, p. 188.

referred to in the first half of Acts. Professionalism,[35] with its emphasis on higher education, degrees and recognised positions, is often the norm in Christian ministry today. As Henri J. M. Nouwen points out, this professionalism can create a power-base, promotes specialisation and suggests separation: 'For many individuals, professional training means power. But ministers, who take off their clothes to wash the feet of their friends, are powerless, and their training and formation are meant to enable them to face their own weakness without fear and make it available to others. It is exactly this creative weakness that gives the ministry its momentum'.[36] Professionalism stands in sharp contrast to the lay movement driven by personal engagement and conviction.

Although formal structures were few, Michael Green argues that leadership seems to be strong and clear in Acts.[37] Through Peter, and later through Paul, the church had a clear direction for its ministry. Copying the model of the synagogues, local leadership was delegated to elders as churches were planted in increasing numbers. Although the centre of influence was moved from Jerusalem to Antioch, there was always a clear direction for the church. This observation must be held in balance with the tensions that were between Jew and gentile Christians on lifestyle issues and the organic way in which the movement grew. Ideological issues were complicated. Paul's epistles also show evidence of this leadership as he teaches on theological issues and gives instruction on practical living.

---

[35] Henri J.M. Nouwen, *Creative Ministry* (New York: Bantam, Doubleday, Dell, 1978), pp. 3–5. Nouwen notes in his introduction 'An ever-growing separation between professionalism and spirituality.' This separation is there in the training of ministers in seminaries and the way the ministry is viewed by boards, leaders and lay-people. The removal of spiritual exercises from the required curriculum in seminaries, lead to a theology without God and/or without spiritual experiences.

[36] Ibid., pp. 115–116.

[37] Green, *30 Years That Changed the World*, pp. 207–201.

Paul shared his leadership. Barnabas, Silas, Timothy, Titus and Luke are some of his co-workers who at times travelled on their own and taught in the churches. Leadership was given to people who proved themselves worthy through results. When the gifts of the Spirit was demonstrated in someone's life and bore fruit, that person was given more responsibility.[38] Recognition came through observed fruits and not from any formal qualification. The Pauline epistles do not seem to be concerned with positions or offices, but rather with function.[39] Even the leadership gifts were seen as a serving function in the church to be used for the good of the community as a whole and not for the position of any particular person.[40] Pettis writes that leadership is not given because of position, but taken because of relevance, and additionally, that authority comes from listening to the times.[41]

Early Christian leaders had to demonstrate entrepreneurship and creativity. The gospel was going to a wider population which culturally was in a totally different place than the one in Judea. Both theology and ministry approaches had to be adjusted. Frost and Hirsh make an interesting observation about leadership in the early church. From the five leadership roles listed in Ephesians 4.11 they discuss at length[42] the APETP model (Apostle, Prophet, Evangelist, Teacher and Pastor) for shared leadership. They note that in a young movement the roles of apostle, prophet and evangelist are strong, whereas in a settled church structure the roles of teacher and pastor tend to be prominent.[43] Apostles and prophets are going new places, establishing new structures, and challenging the establishment. The evangelists are the brave public and private promoters who brings people into the movement. In a settled traditional setting, where maintaining the

---

[38] Ibid., p. 210.
[39] Michael Harper, *Let My People Grow: Ministry and Leadership in the Church* (London: Hodder and Stoughton, 1977), pp. 42–43.
[40] Frost and Hirsch, *The Shaping of Things to Come*, pp. 166–168.
[41] Gallagher and Hertig, *Mission in Acts*, pp. 250–251.
[42] Frost and Hirsch, *The Shaping of Things to Come*, pp. 165–180.
[43] Ibid., p. 178.

status quo has become the norm, teachers and pastors tend to be the stronger leadership roles. Caring for the flock and continuing teaching a traditional message keeps most people happy. Any church can give itself the litmus-test of what kind of leadership it has and conclude what that says about their progression. Many churches would need to pray for more apostles, prophets and evangelists. [44]

The structures for ministry and evangelism also carried the characteristics of a new movement: low cost, simple and personal methods were used. Homes of converts often became the meeting places for the young church. This is documented from the early days in Jerusalem by Acts 2.41-48, but is also as churches were established throughout the Middle East (e.g. Philippi in Acts 16.40). The closeness of the home and the gathering around the table drew Christians together. Commenting Acts 2.41-48, Santos Yao points out the significance of the shared meal in an Asian setting, being a statement of friendship, mutual acceptance, trust and community. He also notes the 'remarkable openness in the early church' and the 'impressive evangelistic influence from the temple and home fellowships in Jerusalem'.[45] By worshipping in homes early Christians could offer a unique sense of belonging and intimacy. The breaking of the bread had strong religious, spiritual and social meanings.

In the informal setting of the house churches pastoral care could be provided in a simple, but effective, way. The needs of the members of the group was easily observed and steps were taken to provide for

---

[44] There is strength in the tight structures of Adventist government. There is order and certainty. That can be illustrated by an almost 1000 page *Working Policy* among unnumbered other manuals and policies. The church stands in danger of administering the present and conserving the past so well that there is no room for the future. The church may forget its own rebellious and radical past under the inspiration of the Spirit, and by so forgetting, deny present generations of young people to approach their current culture with a relevant and renewed approach. *Working Policy of the General Conference of the Seventh-Day Adventist Church*, 2010-2011 Edition (Hagerstown, MD: Review & Herald, 2010).

[45] Santos Yao, 'Dismantling Social Barriers through Table Fellowship' in Gallagher and Hertig, *Mission in Acts*, pp. 31–33.

spiritual, physical or social needs. Thus evangelism happened through fellowship – not only through programmes of persuasion. The very life of the Christian community became a witnessing and including factor. Mary Hinkle underlines the importance of the close fellowships built in the early church: 'In this narrative of life and mission in the early church, Jesus' story is being enacted by the apostles and the communities to which they preach. It comes true in their lives'.[46] A successful attempt to create a similar attractive milieu for sharing the gospel today has been done through the "Alpha seminar." In that programme eating, sharing, teaching and caring all become natural ingredients of the social group. House meetings and groups are still effective means by which to create trust, share faith and care for one another.[47] Looking at the current population in Denmark with its scepticism towards the established churches, the informal, low commitment model of the house group, seems attractive.

Another aspect of the house fellowships is that they represented "neutral ground." Michael Green writes extensively on this issue,[48] arguing that the church must move out of its buildings and meet people where there are no strings attached and no commitment to be made. He takes this thought from the house churches and shows how the apostles spoke publicly in market places (Acts 17.17), school halls (Acts 18.9) and theatres (Acts 17.22) where people were used to come and go. The neutral element was also in the content of the preaching. From the short summaries of the apostles' sermons in Acts, it can be seen that they were all different and related to the culture and needs of the listeners. Paul's at Areopagus (Acts 17) was very different from what he did in Pisidian Antioch (Acts 13) or in Lystra (Acts 14). Still, in all places he met the needs of the people who were there. That is

---

[46] Mary Hinkle, 'Preaching for Mission: Ancient speachies and Postmodern sermons', in Gallagher and Hertig, *Mission in Acts*, p. 100.
[47] Green, *30 Years That Changed the World*, pp. 117–119.
[48] Ibid., pp. 126, 152.

incarnational. Preaching should show the relevance of the story of God in the life of the listener.[49]

The story of Acts also shows the importance of the personal element in evangelism. Visitation, meeting with one individual at the time, was something both Jesus and the apostles practiced. Influence is much stronger in a conversation between two people than in a public speech. When sharing and mutual listening is taking place, growth and change can happen.[50] Also at this junction one cannot but stop to reflect on current evangelistic efforts which are programme- rather than people-oriented. So-called "outreach" is planned in committees without thought for specific individuals. These programmes are executed by professionals, often detached from the lives and witness of other Christians. There are many lessons in the simple approach of the early church where the individual and his/her place in the fellowship stood in the centre. People came to faith by living in the community and by belonging.

Of particular importance to this study is to notice that mission is incarnational.[51] This term is used to describe the idea that in order to enter a culture or a community with the gospel, the church will have to understand, and to a large extent be a part of that community. The church has to meet people where they are. The apostle Paul lived according to this principles as he went from place-to-place teaching

---

[49] Hinkle asks in 'Preaching for Mission', 97: 'Are the speeches in Acts exemplary for postmodern preaching? The speeches are different enough from one another that they resist attempts to develop from them a template for apostolic preaching, either in terms of form or content. Yet they do shape our imagination for the task of preaching In the book of Acts to preach is (1) to tell the story of God's interaction with creation, with Israel and with Jesus, (2) so that hearers may experience in themselves their world in terms of the story and (3) respond in ways that bear witness to the promises God has fulfilled for them in Jesus'.

[50] Green, *30 Years That Changed the World*, pp. 130–131, 137–138.

[51] The use of the term incarnational has its origin in the church's doctrine about Christ. He was one with God but took on human form in order to be one of humankind. He was incarnated—literally remade "in flesh" (John 12.1-3, 14; Phil 2.5-11). God's act in coming to the world as a human being illustrates the need in mission to be one with the people you want to reach.

and planting churches. He outlines his thoughts in 1 Corinthians 9.19-23: 'I have become all things to all men so that by all possible means I might save some. I do all this for the sake of the gospel, that I may share in its blessings'. The church ought to think about mission with this perspective in mind. Ellen G. White, pioneer of the Adventist Church, noted this as she reflected on the missionary lessons to be learned from the incarnation of Christ:

> It is not always pleasant for our brethren to live where the people need help most; but their labors would often be productive of far more good if they would do so. They ought to come close to the people, sit with them at their tables, and lodge in their humble homes. The laborers may have to take their families to places not at all desirable; but they should remember that Jesus did not remain in the most desirable places. He came down to earth that he might help those who needed help.[52]

In *The Forgotten Ways* Hirsch discusses the incarnational nature of ministry, lifestyle and mission. He states that God made a 'radical identification with all that it means to be human',[53] and that this is an example of how Christians have to identify with the people they want to reach. He presents four dimensions of the incarnation as God became a human being in Jesus. He then uses the same dimensions to describe the Christian witness in a community: presence, proximity, powerlessness and proclamation.[54] Living within a specific community or culture, Christians are able to share the gospel in a more natural and relevant way. This does not mean, however, that Christians enter

---

[52] Ellen G. White, *Historical Sketches of the Foreign Missions of the Seventh-day Adventists* (Basel: Imprimerie Polyglotte, 1886), p. 148.
[53] Alan Hirsch, *The Forgotten Ways: Reactivating the Missional Church* (Grand Rapids, MI: Brazos Press, 2006), p. 133.
[54] Ibid., pp. 133–134. A brief explanation of these four concepts highlights: Presence: 'become part of the very fabric of a community;' Proximity: be 'actively involved in the lives of people;' Powerlessness: use Jesus's model of 'servanthood and humility;' Proclamation: 'share the gospel story with those within our world.'

a culture totally on the premises of that culture. The gospel always challenges the practices of any culture. All cultures are to some extent marred by harmful and sinful elements. So in a sense the Christian witness is also prophetic, speaking God's will into a community.[55]

Reflections on Ephesians
In Christ

Ephesians is strongly *christological*. As Stott expresses, 'The Lord Jesus Christ dominates Paul's mind and fills his vision. It seems almost as if he feels compelled to bring Jesus Christ into every sentence he writes, at least in the beginning of his letter'.[56] The phrase "in Christ" is key (1.1; 2.6, 7, 10, 13; 3.6, 21), particularly in the first three chapters with its doctrinal discussions on new life in Christ and the church. "In Christ" brings several outcomes to the Christian individual and community:[57] all blessings of the Father has come to the believers (1.3), God's plan for them becomes real (1.11) and those who have been dead in their sins are made alive (2.5).[58] In Christ the believer has entered a new relationship with the Triune God[59] as a gift and thus also become a part of the fellowship of the church. The second part of Ephesians (chapters 4-6; 2.10) emphasises the new relationships and ethical lifestyle which become a reality for the person who is in Christ. (In this latter part the emphasis tends to be more on the Spirit of Christ than Christ himself.) Bonhoeffer notes that the new Christians were not only asked to believe that Jesus was the Messiah; they were invited to be part of a new community and to take on a new lifestyle. This fresh experience of thinking and living

---

[55] Paul G. Hiebert, *Anthropological Insights for Missionaries* (Grand Rapids, MI: Baker Academic, 1986), pp. 171–192.
[56] Stott, *The Message of Ephesians*, p. 28.
[57] Harold W. Hoehner, *Ephesians: An Exegetical Commentary* (Grand Rapids, MI: Baker Academic, 2002), pp. 171–172.
[58] J.A. Allan, 'The 'In Christ' Formula in Ephesians', *New Testament Studies*, 5 (1958), 58–59.
[59] Allen Verhey and Joseph S. Harvard, *Ephesians* (Louisville, KY: Westminster/John Knox Press, 2011), p. 145.

was seen as a new life in Christ.[60] It is important to note that the relationship to Christ is primary – it comes before changed behaviour and belonging to the community. The latter emerges from the former.

The church

The individuals who put their trust in Christ are unified with the universal church, not so much by their conscious choice, but by default because they belong to Christ. Entrance into the church does not come by membership but by being in Christ. Being in Christ brings radical change in a person's life (4.25-5.20). Paul describes the before (2.13) and the now (2.4-6) as a movement from death to life (2.5-6), from darkness to light (4.18; 5.6-11) and from being far off to come near (2.13, 17, 19). The new believer becomes a part of the church by being transformed and through participation (4.25 to 5.20). These are not prerequisites, but consequences, of belonging. The church thus becomes a new humanity (2.15) which is closely linked to Christ[61] that it is called His body (1.22-23), and the temple in which the Spirit of Christ lives (2.21-22). This new temple replaces the temple in Jerusalem as the dwelling place of God. This spiritual reality is demonstrated by Jean-Claude Verrecchia in his late volume *God of No Fixed Address*, where he explains how Paul moves God's dwelling place from structures and buildings to people.[62] The Jerusalem temple created division but this new temple is open for all who want to enter into fellowship with Christ. In this new 'household of God' (2.19) – substituting the role of Israel in redemption history – there is unity with people of all backgrounds because all belong to Christ (2.16;

---

[60] Dietrich Bonhoeffer, *Life Together* (New York: Harper and Row, 1954), pp. 23–25.

[61] George Eldon Ladd, *A Theology of the New Testament* (Grand Rapids, MI: Eerdmans, 1974), p. 545. 'Paul uses the metaphor of the body to express the oneness of the church with her Lord. . . . The primary emphasis of the metaphor is the unity of believers with Christ; but Paul introduces the concept both in Romans and Corinthians to deal with the problem of Christians' relation to each other.'

[62] Jean-Claude Verrecchia, *God of No Fixed Address. From Altars to Sanctuaries, Temples to Houses* (Eugene, OR: Wipf & Stock, 2015). See particularly Itinerary 1 of part two, pp. 90-103.

3.6). Christ is both the head (1.22-23) and the cornerstone (2.20-22) of the church, thus being the leading entity for its life and the guiding reference point which keeps the whole structure together.

If, from a biblical perspective, belonging to Christ is the criterion for belonging to the universal church, that has consequences for church government. Adrian Peck in his case studies describing two growing churches, Christchurch London and Kingsgate Community Church in Peterborough,[63] noted a philosophy of ministry and church government that marked a difference between a "centre set" and a "bounded set" concept of church. The ideas comes from Paul Hiebert: 'A centre set model as being based on 'intrinsic rather than extrinsic characteristics,' such that one's relationship to a defined centre, based on movement away or towards that centre, determines whether a person is a member of the set. This is not a boundary-free system as 'there is a clear division between things moving in and those moving out.' For a church the centre is Jesus'.[64]

In the mentioned churches belonging was defined by movement towards the centre; which was Christ, the gospel and the basic values of the kingdom of God as outlined by Jesus. These churches had created a vocabulary and simple rituals to acknowledge and affirm a person's belonging and commitment – even if not a formal member. These churches also had "levels" of membership indicating levels of involvement in that particular local church, but these categories

---

[63] Adrian Peck, *Church Growth In Britain: A Thematic Analysis of Two Growing British Churches,* MA Dissertation (Binfield: Newbold College of Higher Education, 2014). See particularly chapter 7, 80-95.

[64] Adrian Peck, *Church Growth In Britain,* p. 80, referring to Paul G. Hiebert, 'The Category 'Christian' in the Mission Task,' *International Review of Mission,* 72 (1983), 423. Paul Hiebert, first applied social set theory to churches. The same focus is expressed by Frost and Hirsch. They speak about an 'ecclesiology entirely on missional grounds,' which is incarnational rather than attractional so that the church becomes 'instinctively centrifugal not centripetal,' Frost and Hirsch, *The Shaping of Things to Come,* xi, pp. 12, 41.

were not defining a person as "in" or "out." Involvement in church ministries was another confirming factor.

Some traditional churches, including the Adventist Church, tend to be "bounded set." They have certain established doctrinal statements and behaviour codes that must be accepted before membership can be granted. This membership is often the requirement for involvement. In light of the "in Christ" message of Ephesians the bounded-set model is seriously challenged. The models for membership and requirements for baptism (which often go together) in the Adventist Church were established in a time when most new members were faithful, believing Christians of other denominations who accepted the Adventist doctrinal understandings and wanted to join that church.

In present times when so many are biblically illiterate and come to the church fellowship with a totally different background, the Adventist Church could benefit from changing its rites of passage. One solution would be to baptise new believers as soon as they have come to faith in Christ, irrespective of an understanding of the most important Adventist teachings. Such a practice would come into tension with the strong emphasis on doctrines in the Adventist Church. Another solution would be to introduce a ceremony which marks a person's initial commitment to Christ and confirms the importance of that decision. The church would do well to publicly recognise a person's step into faith in Christ in a service where his or her faith is affirmed, statements of inclusiveness are made, prayers for the new believer are offered and emphasis is put on the journey ahead. The new cultural context challenges the church's traditional positions on baptism and membership. Leaders would profit from developing an inclusive vocabulary which does not divide people into "them" and "us". Recognising faith and Christian growth as processes and including all who are on a journey in the same direction will create room and acceptance in which individuals can grow in their own way.

Unity in Spirit

The unity discussed in Ephesians is first of all the unity of Jews and gentiles (2.14-22). To divide humanity into two categories seems strange, but is understandable from the Jewish background where Israel was seen as exclusively the people of God. Other religious groups make the same arbitrary division: "us" and "all the others." The unifying element in Ephesians is Christ who has brought down the walls of division (2:14). In him all of God's people are placed in one category: those who have been chosen (1:4-5) and redeemed (1:7). Paul explains in more detail elsewhere that all dividing walls have been taken down bringing Jew and gentile, slave and free, male and female into one in Christ (Gal 3.28; 1 Cor 12.13).

The church in Acts apparently had a very generous inclusiveness in their community. This is shown by the practices described in Acts 2.41-48 where there were close house-fellowships with the breaking of bread, prayers, eating and the sharing of property and financial resources. In this fellowship, which some would call the ideal description of a church, there was joy and care. According to Ephesians, the unity of the church seems to go beyond the immediate members of the group. In Christ all human beings were seen as brothers and sisters and fellowship and responsibility also went to the "neighbours" (4.25).[65] This universal approach is linked to the eternal purposes of God to bring all of creation together in unity under Christ (1.10). The church is an agent for this process of unity and reconciliation of all things.

The Unity in Christ presented in Ephesians seem to be defined as a continuum rather that in a model which classify people as "in" or "out." It appears to be closer to the centre set model than the bounded set model discussed above. In this pattern of thinking people are

---

[65] Paul expresses this as he admonishes Christians to care for the poor, show Christian love in all circumstances and live respectably among non-believers. In this way the Christian community goes beyond the "membership."

judged more on the direction of their journeys than the place they are in at the moment. The church needs to ask itself whether its policies encourage people to continue moving in the right direction without giving them a sense of being an outsider until they reach a point defined by others as sufficient for membership.

Besides having a revelatory role (3.5) and strengthening Christians (3.16), the key role of the Spirit in Ephesians is to create unity (3.5; 4.4). Ephesians contains eight

Trinitarian passages (1.4-14, 17; 2.18, 22; 3.4-5, 14-17; 4.4-6; 5.18-20), and is by some called the Trinitarian letter.[66] The three persons of the Godhead work together for the redemptive purpose. Through the Spirit every Christian becomes connected to this divine fellowship. The work of the Spirit is strongly connected to the work of reconciliation as all who are in Christ have access to the Father through the same spirit (2.16-18). The Spirit has revealed this mystery that all are heirs to the promises (3.6). The Spirit is instrumental in both individual and corporate growth[67] as the power of Christ (3.14-19).

The Spirit has a particularly strong place in the second half of the epistle where personal relationships and ethics are discussed. Michael Green notes that whereas in Acts the Spirit has a corporate function, in the epistles the Spirit is working more on an individual level.[68] Paul describes changes that happen when people live for the new paradigm "in Christ." Whatever stage a person is on they seem to be regarded as being in Christ. There seems to be a trust in what the Trinitarian God is doing in individual lives. Church leadership does not need to monitor each person and see if they are making the right progress (although Paul gives advice on what to do when people live in open

---

[66] Harold W. Hoehner, *Ephesians: An Exegetical Commentary* (Grand Rapids, MI: Baker Academic, 2002), p. 108.
[67] Walter L. Liefeld, *Ephesians* (Downers Grove, IL: InterVarsity Press, 1997), p. 23.
[68] Green, *30 Years That Changed the World*, p. 260.

rebellion against the law of God in 1 Cor 5). There is a trust in the individual's integrity and personal transformation with the help of the Spirit under the headship of Christ. There will be an "ongoing process of assimilation, unity and maturity."[69]

This issue relates strongly to the individualistic mentality of the Danish society today where people want to take responsibility for their own choices and make steps forward according in their own preferred pace. The church and its leaders will have to consider how to guide new individuals "in Christ" in the process of transformation and participation without interfering in the convert's "space" and personal decisions. Reflecting on the above one can ask if the Adventist Church can operate in line with such values and principles. Even if there is a tradition for a very clearly defined line between who is a real Adventist and who is not, the church can with well-directed effort modify that approach through clear value-based messages from leadership. Through teaching, preaching, new practices, the presentation of different values and the use of different language a more generous and open atmosphere can be established. There are forces in Adventism that want to keep a model where all new members must fit a certain description but it is my conviction that most of the membership in the church in Denmark is ready for a more open model that includes people on different stages of the Christian walk. This places a heavy responsibility on leaders, which will be addressed in the last chapter.

---

[69] Liefeld, *Ephesians*, p. 23.

CHAPTER 6

Perspectives on change

This chapter continues theological reflection in order to demonstrate that throughout the history of the people of God, in Bible times and in the experience of the church, change has always taken place, can be expected and must be welcomed. As this study recommends changes and adjustments to the ministries of the Adventist Church, some readers may question the correctness of moving away from practices established under God's guidance. The following material, though limited, establishes that, although the fundamental principles of the people's lives with God will stay the same throughout history, their application may change according to local circumstances.

Different times ask for different types of leadership, organisation, teachings and prophetic ministries. Two biblical examples are examined. The first surveys worship in the Old Testament, and the second reflects on the comprehensive changes the early church went through when it moved from being a Jewish "sect" to a worldwide movement.[1] Change is part of the life of the people of God. Observations on changes in ministry of the Danish Adventist Church will follow. The last section of this chapter summarises key lessons learned by key leaders of three church plants where new approaches to ministry and evangelism have proved successful.

---
[1] These changes were discussed to some extent in chapter 5, so only brief additional reflections will be made in this chapter.

Worship in the Old Testament

The Bible presents a unity of thought in many overarching themes. At the same time it describes a large variety of practices and understandings, varying with change of time, location and culture. One such area is worship as described in the Old Testament.[2]

The patriarchs lived in extended families including servants and slaves. They were nomads, moving according to the needs of their flocks. A household could be of significant sise. Abraham was able to assemble 'three hundred eighteen trained men born in his household' (Gen 14.14) when he went on a mission to rescue Lot and his family. Worship was organised within the context of these extended families. The building of an altar or the marking of a particular spot as sacred was common. Abraham built altars and made sacrifices in relation to important events in his life; for instance at Shechem where God appeared to him and promised his descendants the land (Gen 12.7) and when he camped and worshipped at Bethel (Gen 12.8). He returned to his altars later for worship (Gen 13.3-4; 13.18). Abraham's son, Isaac, followed the same practice (Gen 26.25).

Jacob, Abraham's grandson, set up a stone to memorialise his spiritual experience at Bethel (Gen 28.16-22). The altars seem to have been physical reminders of encounters with God (Gen 35.1-7), and remained important places of worship in Jewish history. These places marked the reality of personal decisions and commitments. George Buttrick writes: 'Israelite worship in Genesis is, however rudimentary, personal and family related'.[3] *The Harper's Bible Dictionary* provides this summary of patriarchal worship: 'The worship practiced by the patriarchs knows nothing of all this [the rituals of the later temple]. Their worship was simple and informal; they had no priests or temples. Rather, the patriarchs themselves offered burnt offerings at

---

[2] Jean-Claude Verrecchia, *God of No Fixed Address*. This volume gives an oversight over, and reflects on, places of worship in the Scriptures.

[3] George Arthur Buttrick, *Interpreter's Dictionary of the Bible*, Vol. 4 (Nashville, TN: Abingdon Press, 1962), p. 879.

temporary altars they built themselves in the open... In later periods this would probably have been considered idolatrous'.[4]

There is nothing documented about Israelite worship patterns in the time of slavery in Egypt, but from the early chapters of Exodus it can be gathered that there was a common memory of the God of Abraham, Isaak and Jacob (3.6, 15-18; 4.27-31). After the Exodus the people of Israel built a tabernacle in the desert (Exod 25.8-9; chapters 25-31). The tabernacle was a place where God would "dwell" and it became the central place for worship. Aaron and the Levites were set aside as priests (Exod 28.1-4; Num 1.50-53). Worship became a national matter. The authority of the Levites and the temple was extended beyond religious matters to numerous civil functions. Personal faith and decisions might have been similar to that of the patriarchal period, but the external practice of worship was radically different.

The patterns of life changed significantly for the people of Israel as they settled in Canaan. Now that they had become farming and herding people, living in villages, towns and small cities, worship practices also changed. The tabernacle of the desert wandering was placed in Shiloh (Josh 18.1-10) and was no longer just the central point of a camp: 'Levites were considered to be the proper people to act as priest (Judg 17.13) but individual Israelites continued to offer their own sacrifices on simple outdoor altars (Judg 6:.24-27; 13.19)'.[5] There are references to worship and local shrines in Dan, Gilgal, Bethel, Beersheba, Shechem and Shilo.[6] This Time of the judges seems to have included private worship practices similar to those in the era of the patriarchs. There were, however, still some residual elements of tabernacle worship in the desert. The story about

---

[4] Paul J Achtemeier, *Harper's Bible Dictionary* (San Francisco: Harper and Row, 1985), pp. 1145–1146.

[5] Achtemeier, *Harper's Bible Dictionary*, p. 1146.

[6] Buttrick, *Interpreter's Dictionary of the Bible*, p. 880.

Samuel's family (1 Samuel 1-3) indicates that visits to the tabernacle and the celebration of the festivals continued.

The nation of Israel was more firmly established after a king was chosen. Through Saul's and David's war victories a period of prosperity and peace arrived. During his reign Solomon built a magnificent temple in Jerusalem (1 Chr 6.32; 1 Kings 6-8). Worship in Israel was again centralised. The inauguration of the temple was made "official" by the presence of all civil leaders of the land, and large portions of the population travelled to Jerusalem for the festivities (1 Kings 8; 2 Chr 5).[7] Worship in other places was discouraged. Particularly during the reforms under Josiah, there was a strong drive to get rid of all other places of worship[8] and have the "true worship" of God in the temple in Jerusalem (2 Kings 23.8-15). When Israel was divided the northern tribes established worship places in Bethel and Dan (1 Kings 12.26-33).

The periods of the Assyrian (722 BC) and Babylonian (586 BC)[9] exiles again changed the conditions for worship. The temple in Jerusalem was destroyed around 586 BC and large portions of the population were moved to other parts of the Middle East. The temple had represented the presence of the Lord, and his nearness had to be understood in a different way in exile (Ezek 1.1; 11.16). Without the temple the priesthood and the sacrifices were no longer at the centre of worship. Prayers and readings, teaching and fellowship became essential aspects of worship, and the smaller group became more significant. Some factors indicate that the earliest roots of the

---

[7] It is of interest to note how strange, and probably disgusting, this worship ceremony would appear to a modern worshipper. Still, it was acceptable to the Lord at that time.

[8] It should be noted that the worship at different sites in Israel was often worship of local gods and thus was seen as idolatry (1 Kings 14.23-24; 15.3-4,14). This is true both for the period of the judges and that of the kings. Madeleine Sweeny Miller, *Black's Bible dictionary* (London: A. and C. Black, 1973), p. 825.

[9] T. Desmond Alexander and Brian S Rosner, *New Dictionary of Biblical Theology* (Downers Grove, IL: InterVarsity Press, 2000), p. 476.

synagogue lie in the religious practices of the exile,[10] although actual proof is hard to come by.[11] Throughout the Old Testament there are references to people doing worship, but the records demonstrate that the form of worship varied significantly.

The gospel to the gentiles

The most significant change in the history of the Christian church took place when the early church moved from being a Jewish community in Jerusalem and Judea to becoming a cross-cultural movement including peoples of many cultures. The disciples grew up as Jews, were disciples of Jesus in a Jewish context, and were faced with a mission challenge they were only partly (if at all) prepared for. The New Testament gives numerous references to the tension in the early church about issues which relate to that challenge.[12] They bear witness to the need for drastic change in religious establishments when they become too comfortable and complacent in their own traditions.

Peter, and eventually the whole leadership, changed their theological positions on some points (Acts 11.18) because of God's actions through dreams and guidance. One new understanding was that God cares for all human beings, and that he does not see any human being as "impure or unclean,"[13] and a second understanding was the scope of the mission task of the church. These significant

---

[10] J. D Douglas and N Hillyer, *New Bible Dictionary* (Leicester: InterVarsity Press, 1982), p. 1142.

[11] Bruce M Metzger, Michael David Coogan, *The Oxford Companion to the Bible* (New York: Oxford University Press, 1993), p. 722.

[12] Examples: Acts 15: to what extent should gentile Christians be expected to keep the Torah?; Acts 10 and 11: should gentiles be viewed as equals to Jews?; Luke 4.24-30: does God really care about the people of other nations?; 1 Cor 9.19-23: is there room for different lifestyles and practices in the church?

[13] Peter emphasises this point several times, as he enters Cornelius' house and then after visiting for some time (Acts 10.28, 34-35) and before the elders in Jerusalem (Acts 11.12-18).

changes in theology and mission did not come from a strategic committee or from one strong leader or even a leadership team. It was Christ, through the Holy Spirit, who facilitated the changes.

When commenting on the radical changes that happened in the early church, Ray Anderson states, 'The church does not emerge out of its past'. He emphasises that in times of radical change and paradigm shifts, Christ, through the Spirit, leads the church into changes it could not have perceived or organised by itself. Only the Spirit who knows the future can lead the church into the future.[14] The role of church leadership in this case was to recognise what God was doing and then follow and implement that change.[15] Reflecting further on new situations, Hirsh discusses the place of uncertainty and chaos in the Christian ministry and notes that the church tends to settle for the middle-class values of comfort and convenience, safety and security.[16] He states that 'equilibrium is death' and makes the following challenging statement:

> What is it about disequilibrium that seems to stimulate life and energy? And what is it about stability that seems to stifle it? . . . Is it because life itself is unpredictable and chaotic and that when we establish organisations that seek to control and minimise the

---

[14] Anderson, *An Emergent Theology for Emerging Churches*, p. 84.

[15] Adventist writer, Ellen White, comments on this significant event: 'When the brethren in Judea heard that Peter had gone to the house of a gentile and preached to those assembled, they were surprised and offended. They feared that such a course, which looked to them presumptuous, would have the effect of counteracting his own teaching. When they next saw Peter they met him with severe censure, saying, 'Thou wentest in to men uncircumcised, and didst eat with them.' . . . Peter laid the whole matter before them. . . . On hearing this account, the brethren were silenced. Convinced that Peter's course was in direct fulfillment of the plan of God, and that their prejudices and exclusiveness were utterly contrary to the spirit of the gospel, they glorified God, saying, 'Then hath God also to the gentiles granted repentance unto life.' Thus, without controversy, prejudice was broken down, the exclusiveness established by the custom of ages was abandoned, and the way was opened for the gospel to be proclaimed to the gentiles.' Ellen G. White, *The Acts of the Apostles*, pp. 141-142.

[16] Hirsch, *The Forgotten Ways*, p. 43.

dangers of life, these organisations in the end stifle it? The history of missions is quite clear about this: Christianity is at its very best when it is at the more chaotic fringes. It is when the church settles down, and moves away from the edge of chaos, that things go awry.[17]

The aftermath of the episode with Peter and Cornelius included the council in Jerusalem, as described in Acts 15. The discussion was whether or not the new gentile Christians should be circumcised and keep the laws of Moses. With a few exceptions the answer was negative. The result was that gentile Christians had a different lifestyle from their Jewish fellow believers.[18] Tensions in the early church over lifestyle differences did not go away quickly. References to them are made throughout the New Testament.

These two brief surveys of biblical issues, show significant change of practice and emphasis over time. It sets a pattern for understanding God's leading as organic, incarnational and sensitive to context. In the following section focus will be on changes in recent times in the ministry of the Adventist Church.

Changes in Adventist History

The establishment of the Adventist Church marked a dramatic change in itself. The early Adventists came from different Christian backgrounds and often went through painful changes in obedience to their new convictions. The early Adventist Church preached "Present Truth" – a controversial message they saw as particularly relevant to a

---

[17] Ibid., p. 258.

[18] The issue of circumcision is discussed in, for example, Gal 5.2-6; 11-12 and Rom 2.25-29. Some inconsistency can be traced in Paul's behaviour as he allowed Timothy to be circumcised (Acts 16.3). This episode underlines the fact that different situations demand different solutions. The celebration of the Jewish festivals was another issue (Rom 14.5-6; Col 2.16-17; Gal 4.9-11). The festivals seem to have had some significance for the apostles although their observance was not a requirement (Acts 20. 6, 16). Questions about diet arose in 1 Cor 8.1-10; Rom 14.5-6; Col 2.16-17.

particular time. The concept of Present Truth (significantly the name of the church magazine) indicates an understanding that some truth is of particular importance and relevance for a certain time and that present truth is not the same as past truth. The pioneers shared a spirit of reformation, and seem to have been more open to change than what is the case for most of the Adventist Church today.

The following section looks at the health ministries of the Adventist Church in Denmark as an example of the changing nature of mission. These ministries are often called "the right hand" of the message as Adventists see it as a part of their mission to help people get a healthier and better life.[19] Varying circumstances in culture, knowledge, finance, politics, and leadership has brought significant changes to these ministries over the years.

The significance of entrepreneurship, creativity, drive and relevance are demonstrated by the multifaceted ministry of Ottosen (1864-1942),[20] of which a large sanatorium (*Skodsborg Badesanatorium*,

---

[19] The Adventist world headquarters' Home Page gives information about Adventist philosophy and practical advice on healthy living. See Seventh-day Adventists Home Page, http://healthministries.com/ (accessed 3 July 2014). It also provides some statistics of institutions and numbers helped. The Adventist Church focus on health is a response to the idea that the human body is a temple for the Holy Spirit (1 Cor 6.15-16). Eight health principles that the church promotes are: 'Pure air, sunlight, abstemiousness, rest, exercise, proper diet, the use of water, trust in divine power.' These principles are taken from White, *Ministry of Healing*, p. 127.

[20] Ottosen was instrumental in many initiatives. He edited a spiritual magazine for children (*Lys i Hjemmet* [*Light in the Home*], which was published twice a month), wrote extensively in a Danish-Norwegian health magazine and started Skodsborg's own magazine (*Skodsborger samfundet*, internal paper for the institution since 1923). Ottosen established three Sanatoriums (Pedersen, *Syvende Dags Adventistkirken I Danmark*, pp. 85–86), a school for cooks and physiotherapists, and a food factory. The sise and volume of the health related work is seen in the following statistics: In the three Scandinavian countries, where the total membership in 1928 was 8,183 (Secretary, 'Report from the Scandinavian Union', *Missionsefterretninger Fra Norge og Danmark* 9:65 (September 1928), there were 540 workers in the Adventist health institutions, and another 275 workers in private Adventist institutions. The church-owned institutions brought an income of ten million kroner. See conversion table on www.

hereafter: Skodsborg) was the flagship. As a young veterinarian student with poor health, Ottosen came in contact with the Adventist Church in Copenhagen.[21] Brorson told him about the radical treatments and natural remedies of Battle Creek Sanatorium in Michigan[22] (an Adventist institution), and the young Ottosen travelled to the US to learn from Kellogg, head physician and president, who was an internationally known figure then also today for the invention of Kellogg's cornflakes. Ottosen returned to Europe after completing medical school and toured this continent visiting and learning from famous sanatoriums. Strongly motivated he came back to Denmark as a thirty-three year old, and with the blessing of Adventist leaders bought a property north of Copenhagen. Twenty-five years later a series of large buildings[23] with halls for treatment and nice residential rooms had been erected.

Skodsborg, with its state of the art equipment and treatments, became a model for many institutions in Scandinavia – inside and outside of the Adventist Church. Ottosen became a famous speaker and travelled all over Scandinavia lecturing, for substantial fees, on the latest theories defining a healthy lifestyle, and the use of natural remedies both for healing and health improvement. Many famous artists, actors /actresses and people of high society enjoyed the luxury and comfort of the beautiful and extravagant sanatorium. Corresponding to a Christian philosophy, the high income from the wealthy was used to provide free care for the poor.[24]

---

abcnyheter.no/ faktainnhold/diverse/100111/inflasjonsstatistikk (accessed 2 July 2014)) to the church over a period of four years (Secretary, 'Report from the Scandinavian Union', 65).

[21] *Skodsborg Badesanatorium, 1898-1923* (Copenhagen: B. Nielsens bogtrykkeri, n.d.), pp. 3-4.
[22] Ibid., p. 14.
[23] Ibid., 11. Most buildings were built between 1907 and 1923.
[24] *Skodsborger samfundet: 1991-1992 Ultima Versio* (Odense: Dansk Bogforlag 1993), 44-45 and *Skodsborg Badesanatorium, 1898-1923*, p. 9. The statistics show a significant percentage of poor people and pensioners as visitors.

Skodsborg kept growing up to the 1960s when conditions changed for private hospitals. The government promoted state-owned institutions[25] and only paid for treatment outside if there was not enough capacity in these. This change of politics became an increasing challenge for Skodsborg. As long as Ottosen was in charge, up to the late-1930s, and those who had worked with him continued their leadership profile up to the 1960s, the institution grew.[26] Whether it was government policies or the fact that new leaders came in who only managed the institution rather than continuing the entrepreneur spirit, is hard to know, but the growth plateaued in the 1960s, and by the 1980s the institution was no longer state of the art, progressive or, in some people's opinion, working along the philosophy of the church. It had become dependent on the changing winds of politics, and external circumstances seemed to set the agenda.

From being a famous entity in Scandinavia, Skodsborg faded into relative anonymity and finally went bankrupt in 1992. The prosperous years were good and a sad ending does not take that away. Maybe the church could have been more proactive and made strategic moves to adjust to new circumstances. The success story of days past could inspire new initiatives – not repeating the past. True to its convictions about a holistic lifestyle and a ministry of healing, the Adventist Church could look for a niche where the National Health Service does not provide and start a ministry.[27]

A curiosity that might illustrate the need for change in the approach to ministry is the decision from 1934 by the Adventist Church in Denmark to start the production of plant margarine.[28] *Den Sanitære Fødevarefabrik* [the church owned *Health Food Factory*] made a, in those days, radical, creative and progressive move as it presented

---

[25] *Skodsborger samfundet 1991-1992, Ultima Versio*, p. 52.
[26] Ibid., p. 44.
[27] Two such areas would be to address the "epidemic" of loneliness in all age-groups, as increasing numbers are living alone, and the healing of broken families.
[28] *Missionsefterretninger*, 10 (October 1934), 79.

a hopefully healthy alternative to butter. It was a great success, but things gradually change. Through bankruptcy the margarine factory was lost to the church. In 2014, several large manufacturers provide the market with an endless variety of margarines and butters, and the church must recognise that it is not its mission to do this anymore.

A small-scale, private project in the Adventist Church which has been able to adapt to changing circumstances is the *Sundhedsbussen*] [*Health Service Bus*]. Around 1985, a group of young health workers got together, bought a second hand bus and equipped it as a rolling clinic. They parked the bus in market places, gave free health checks and talked to people about lifestyle issues and their health.[29] Volunteers' commitments changed and after about fifteen years it was time to move on. The profile changed and the bus was used to serve food and hand out clothes to the homeless in Copenhagen. The bus got old and worn, and in 2002 it was sold and replaced by a caravan pulled by a car. The ministry for the homeless and drug addicts continued.[30] The vision grew, and a dream was to have permanent presence in Copenhagen with a centre for aid to the needy, service to the local community and possibly a church plant. The idea for the second-hand shop Happy Hand crystalised. The concept was to run a shop on a voluntary basis, sell second-hand items, and pour all the profits back into the community providing for the needy with food and clothing, helping kids from weak families with homework, providing a free counselling service, and do a spiritual ministry.[31] The dream became a reality in 2012 when a shop was opened on one of the busiest streets of Copenhagen.[32] A name that keeps recurring

---

[29] Anne-May Müller, ‚Det er Koldt at være Due', *Adventnyt*, 4 (2005), 12–13.
[30] Inger Falk, ‚Vi Elsker Fordi Han Elskede Først', *Adventnyt*, 6 (2008), 7.
[31] Berit Elkjær, ‚Adventistkirken Åbner Genbrugsbutik På Nørrebro', *Adventnyt*, 4 (2012), 5.
[32] This initiative also shows an effective link between a local initiative and the world headquarters as the project was generously sponsored by funds from the "Mission for the Cities" programme. This initiative was presented at the Annual Council of the General Conference of the Seventh-Day Adventist Church in Silver Springs, October 2011.

through this 30 year story is Berit Elkjær who has been an initiative taker and the driving force.[33] The success continued as members in the north-western parts of Denmark picked up the concept and started the second Happy Hand shop in 2014.[34] The examples above are from ministries run by the church to help people get better lives. They illustrate the changing nature of life and the need to constantly adapt to new circumstances.

Observations from Three Adventist Church Plants

This section will summarise some of the lessons learned from three recent Adventist church plants which have been able to connect to new groups of people. The purpose here is to demonstrate that new ways of doing church have proved successful. The information comes from in-depth interviews with the church leaders. There are limitations to the strength of the evidence from these interviews since they are done only with leaders, but even if the interviews on their own cannot be classified as a full-scale research method,[35] they have been executed according to good practice,[36] and they bring important

---

[33] Berit Elkjær, ,Verdens Bedste Missionsarbejde', *Adventnyt*, 7/8 (2012), 4.
[34] Andreas Müller, '*Happy Hand Udvider i Aalborg*', *Adventnyt*, 2 (2014), 7.
[35] John Swinton and Harriet Mowat, *Practical Theology and Qualitative Research* (London: SCM, 2006). Swinton and Mowat use a definition of qualitative research from J. McLeod, who writes in the context of counselling and therapy: 'Qualitative research is a process of careful, rigorous inquiry into aspects of the social world. It produces formal statements or conceptual frameworks that provide new ways of understanding the world, and therefore comprises knowledge that is practically useful for those who work with issues around learning and adjustment to the pressures and demands of the social world', 31. Qualitative research, e.g. a case study, would demand further gathering of date from different sources; repeated visits to the church plants, the observation of their meetings and publications and interviewing other categories of people.
[36] Overviews of how interviews can and should be conducted can be found in Graham Birley and Neil Moreland, *A Practical Guide to Academic Research* (London: Kogan Page, 1998), pp. 49–51; Jerry Willis, *Foundations of Qualitative Research: Interpretive and Critical Approaches* (Thousand Oaks, CA: SAGE Publications, 2007), pp. 244–247. See also Richard Robert Osmer, *Practical Theology: An Introduction* (Grand Rapids, MI: Eerdmans,

input for our understanding of ministry in a new context.[37] The three churches are The Café Church in Copenhagen,[38] X-preszo in Rotterdam[39] and Viborg International Adventist Church.[40]

2008), pp. 62-63.MI: William B. Eerdmans Pub. Co., 2008 The questions for the interviews referred to here, have been handed in to the supervisor for this dissertation for evaluation. They are not of a sensitive or private character and therefore do not need any approval of an ethical committee. The interviews were recorded on video-camera and stored. The interviewees signed agreements regarding the interview process. These forms were provided by Fuller Theological Seminary. These materials are available from the author.

[37] In the interviews particular focus was placed on the following issues: First, important lessons from establishing the church; second, the church-planters' perception of what connected new believers to their church, and what the new believers found relevant there; third, the importance of relationships and fellowship (small groups) for numerical and spiritual growth; fourth, their emphasis on spirituality, and fifth, reflections on what the Adventist Church at large has to change in order to do mission in Western European culture.

[38] The interviewees from the Café Church in Copenhagen were Susanne Wiik Kalvaag (member from the early beginnings and at present worship leader - SK), Cyril Kalvaag (member from the start and currently elder - CK) and Rebecca Pedersen (member from early in the Café Church history and small group leader from 1999 to 2004, currently pastoring a different church plant - RP). SK and CK were interviewed together by the author via Skype from Fredensborg, 21 August 2013. RP was interview in person by the author in Binfield, 6 September 2013.

[39] The group interview with the leadership team from X-preszo, Rotterdam included people who have been in the church plant from the start–or very close to that: Martin Altink (AT), Marco Beruoets, Renate Hazel (RH), Steven Hazel (Leader, SH), Esther van de Putte (EP), Paul van Putten, and Alexander Trueman. Interview led by the author at Huis ter Heide, the Netherlands, 25 August 2013. The interview was done when I visited with church leadership for a weekend teaching on leadership and spending time on strategic planning. Throughout the weekend, time was spent in informal conversations and for two hours the leadership met together for the semi-structured group interview. That had the format of a "focus group." (Pranee Liamputtong, *Focus Group Methodology: Principle and Practice* (London: SAGE, 2011), pp. 2-3, 42–46, 54.) The focus group is used frequently in social research. See Immy Holloway, *Qualitative Research in Health Care* (Maidenhead: Open University Press, 2005), pp. 55–70, because it is easy to organise, reliable and provides answers to qualitative research questions. Questions were asked in an open-ended manner to bring out, as far as possible, the opinions, observations and insights of the members of the group.

[40] This Skype interview was with Ingelis Hagen Jensen, who has been the key leader for the ministry of that church 12 August 12 2014.

The church in Copenhagen

The Café Church in Copenhagen was planted in the late-1990s and is now an established church. It has been a controversial element in the Adventist Church because of its alternative worship style, music and ministry. The informal services with contemporary music were held in a café setting with people sitting around tables. While controversial, the Café Church was able to attract many people from segments of the population which the Adventist churches normally would not reach. People came from a new age background and young Adventist people, who did not find traditional church relevant. The Café Church had significant growth throughout the years 1999 to 2006. [41]

The terms spirituality and relationships summarise the essence from the interviews, and were the factors which brought people to the church and kept them there. Spirituality was emphasised strongly by all three interviewees from Café Church. A central motive as the church started, was the desire to search for, and know, God. Prayer was given a major place in all aspects of church life, and a significant ministry for intercessory prayer was established. After worship services visitors and members would queue up to be prayed for by experienced leaders.

SK commented: 'In the culture around us people will try anything as long as it works. They pick from all the shelves. You can go to a witch or to intercessory prayer' [my edit from longer passage]. SK also made this observation: 'I believe it connects to today's culture

---

[41] The Café Church's membership has later changed and there has been some decline. There might be important lessons to be learned from that, too. Some changes have come from natural developments like many of the young singles have become married couples with children. The style and ministry has changed accordingly. Sadly, the story of the Café Church has been marred by conflicts, tensions, criticism and attacks. Both key leaders left the plant at a crucial time (2006/2007). Its identity in relationship to the Adventist Church has not always been clear. These are some observation made by myself and further analysis into this would be helpful for future church plants in the denomination.

because in intercessory prayer you are seen – genuinely seen'. The language used up front was strongly spiritual, confirming that God was present. Singing praise songs was an act of worshipping God and moving into a relationship with him. Submission to God was emphasised. Related to this spirituality was a strong emphasis on honesty and authenticity. People were real, sharing good and bad. The deeply spiritual worship services drew many visitors 'like a magnet' RP noted.[42] 'They experienced God there' RP confirmed, and she remembers one visitor with a new age background experiencing that 'Jesus showed up as the biggest [of the spirits]'. SK: 'It is outreach to be super-spiritual today'.

The Café Church was very strategic about building relationships inside and outside the church. Most new visitors were friends, colleagues and acquaintances of people already attending and in that way they had a connection to the church beyond the programme itself. Many church services ended with small group discussions around the tables. This practice became an introduction to house groups which all were encouraged to attend. RP remembers that out of approximately 120 visitors, eighty-five attended a house group. Stronger bonding, spiritual growth and discipleship took place in the groups which had relevant materials, focused leadership and strategic plans. CK mentioned the strong individualism that people brought to the groups, but also that praying and reading the Bible created 'the question in their own mind as to whether they are the central shaft around which the universe is turning. . . . People meet God in prayer'. For the Café Church the small groups did not bring many new visitors to the church services, but established them in the community and helped them to grow.

---

[42] CK noted that when the church started seeker services, with a low-key spirituality, they had to be dropped again because the visitors wanted hard core spirituality.

X-preszo

X-preszo was chosen as an example here because of its ability to reach the average indigenous population and because it was recommended by the coordinator for church planting in the Dutch Union of the Adventist Church.[43] X-preszo was planted in 2005, and the name refers to personal honesty and openness. It holds its informal services with contemporary music in a rented community hall.

Relationships and spirituality summarise the emphasis of the group interview, but in the opposite order from Café Church. Before X-preszo was planted, several of the present leaders had strong networks with non-Christians who met for spiritual conversations and friendship in their homes. The idea to start a church grew out of a need for a place to bring these friends for worship and systematic teaching, realising that most traditional churches would not meet the needs of their friends, nor appeal to them.

X-preszo started with "Matthew-parties" rather than church services. A Matthew party takes its model from the story of the disciple who invited his friends to a party so that they could meet Jesus (Luke 5.27-32). From that philosophy the church started with barbeques, games in the park and other social events for their friends and the community in general. People came just to "hang out" and expressed appreciation for the fellowship and fun: 'You are good people. I want to be with you' (SH). The fellowship in the Matthew parties was not based on a common religious conviction. Anybody was welcome. 'People want to belong, to be included' (SH). The strong emphasis on building community regardless of faith issues, can be illustrated by key words the leadership team used to describe their church: food, relevance, authenticity, relevancy, attention,

---

[43] Recommended by Rudy Dingjan. X-preszo is a church plant in Rotterdam. The Netherlands is reached by a just four-hour drive from Denmark and has a very similar culture. The findings there will be relevant for an understanding of ministry in Denmark.

friendship and acceptance. RH concluded the little brainstorm with the exclamation: 'We accept people as they are – with everything they have. We care'.

This open attitude had been the style of the house fellowships, which carried the name "life groups" because all aspects of life could be talked about. There was 'sharing, laughing and crying'. Individuals were welcomed on their own terms and were not pushed into a programme or a faith. Some did grow into the Christian faith, some did not. This open atmosphere was brought in as X-preszo started worship services. After some initial adjustments, X-preszo have continued their Matthew parties and connected them to their worship time. RH said, 'Some come and hang out. Some are attracted to the spiritual content; some are not. . . We make room for Jesus to do what he does by being relaxed and being ourselves'.

The emphasis on spirituality is strong. SH stated, 'People are attracted to spirituality' and noted, 'Everybody is looking for something. People are searching, but in this modern society, particularly in Holland, [they] are really turned down [off?] by churches, the big organisations . . . like big companies. People are disappointed and suspicious about these organisations . . . They are searching, but through relationships'. 'People are interested in spirituality, but not in denominations. They don't care whether we are Adventist or Pentecostal or whatever'. The working of the Holy Spirit is emphasised in worship, because it is the personal and the spiritual that make the services relevant. RH: 'In the services there is a shower of spirituality . . . We make room for what the Holy Spirit is doing. He is doing it . . . You can see when it is happening to people'. AT: 'When we plan the service, and we feel that the Spirit is leading somewhere else, then we just do it. . . . Before we did not talk so much about Jesus. But now we do it a lot. It is right in your face'. Part of that spirituality is honesty and authenticity. EP commented: 'The worship leader is real. She, or he, also shares pain'.

Viborg International Adventist Church (Denmark)

In 2008, the Adventist Church in Viborg was on the verge of closing with an attendance of six-to-eight and an aging church building. A "re-plant" was started when Ingelis Jensen initiated a new ministry reaching immigrant families. Through social support for both adults and children, she has created a network of people helping each other. The ministries reach immigrants from Asian, African and South-American countries, and include practical help towards integration into Danish society: teaching Danish, often with the Gospels as textbook, teaching Danish customs, helping with the practical use of banks, post-office, the hospital and the like. The helping ministries happen in the homes of the immigrants and strong ties are established. Christian witness and Bible studies often follow as relationships are established. The support is given without view to membership so the network related to the Adventist Church is larger than formal membership. So is attendance. One illustration of this relationship was the Bhutanese family who chose to have a Christian burial service in the Adventist Church.

In 2014 there was an average attendance of forty for the traditional church services in a refurbished church building. Many immigrant children come to the Sabbath school classes (Christian teaching classes) provided for them. In the interview Ingelis Jensen emphasises that it is the network of people, the visits in the homes and the social work of the church that has contributed to this growth.

Deeper reflections on these interviews will be given in chapters 7 and 8. At this junction contrasts to traditional evangelism are noticed. These church plants have a relational approach to people, let each person grow on their own terms – often in small groups, focus is on fellowship and meeting God more than doctrinal positions with an emphasis on belonging. In Viborg the social and supporting element is strong. There are connections to the characteristics of the Danish population.

This chapter has discussed change. The purpose has been to demonstrate that God has led His people in different ways according to different circumstances, and furthermore, that the Christian message has to be understood and lived in a cultural context. The Adventist Church started with radical views which related biblical ideas to issues in North America in the 1800s. Today, the church in Denmark is facing a totally different society. The church will need to rethink its message and the way it communicates it, to be relevant to the present population in Denmark.

PART THREE
MINISTRY STRATEGY

CHAPTER 7

Reaching the current Danish poplulation

The purpose of this study has been to understand developments in Danish culture and to reflect on how these changes affect the ministry and mission of the Adventist Church. Changes that strongly relate to faith, beliefs, spirituality and relationships to church organisations have been emphasised. An attempt to analyse and understand such a complex picture is a challenging endeavour. Many elements are beyond one's full understanding and the changing nature of culture makes an absolute analysis difficult. What one attempts to describe today may be slightly out of date in the near future. Human beings cannot be put in boxes. The Holy Spirit works in ways that go beyond what scholars can put into categories. Therefore, the reflections below are written in humility, recognising that there are genuine limitations to understanding. Admittedly, the ambition to cover such a large number of issues was high, still some clear clues have emerged. Many of the characteristics of the present population point in the direction of relational ministries in smaller contexts of groups and networks.

The task now is to take those critical characteristics of Danish society outlined in chapters 2 and 3 and explore further the implications for the mission of the Adventist Church. The observations made through the research probably support what many people know intuitively, still it is helpful to document some of the facts that move general observations into more solid positions.

As noted in chapter 2, about 3 percent of Denmark's population are Christians in a traditional, Bible-believing sense, holding a traditional Christian worldview as well as accepting classic Christian doctrines. Over the years these types of people have made up the main recruitment category for the Adventist Church as most new members have come from other Christian denominations. My opinion is that if this small segment was to become the sole target of evangelism in the Adventist Church, the church would fail to follow the Great Commission given by Jesus. He stated that His followers should 'go and make disciples of all nations' (Matt 28.19). The task of the church must be to reach the great variety of people in the Danish population.

Given the habits of thinking in the Danish population and the current trends in the Danish Adventist Church it is difficult to have any easy optimism about the future, but there are opportunities the church can grasp and move on to a better future. The church will have to face and tackle the challenges and use the opportunities in order to be true to Jesus's commission. As far as I can see the Adventist Church has these three options: first: be radical in implementing new methods and new ways to present the gospel. This might estrange and upset long time and traditional members and create conflict. Second, simply cater for current members and become more and more out of touch with present culture thereby finding membership and attendance dwindling. Finally, a combination of the two which seems at best difficult, but might become a reality by doing the progressive moves in new church plants and pilot projects. This will be discussed some more in the last chapter on ministry model.

Only a brief summary follows as a backdrop for further reflections below. Secularisation, pluralism, individualism, postmodernism and a new spirituality are terms that describe deep changes in the Danes' relationship to faith issues. People are more spiritual now than thirty years ago, although less religious in the meaning of adhering to a belief system. Each individual is expected to believe on their own terms as "self" has become the major reference point. Many believe in something which they cannot define, and are seeking experiences of the supernatural and for meaning. While large church organisations often are seen as operating out of self-interest, the personal conversation with other authentic individuals is welcomed. Experience and practical usability is attractive to individuals with this personalised spirituality who tend to ask "Does it work?" and "Is it important?" rather than "Is it true?" Many find a church that does the right thing more attractive than one that is teaching the right doctrines.

In response to this, the Adventist Church may have to define its ministry and identity less in terms of what it thinks and more in terms of what it is and does.[1] Church members also could profit from seeing others as fellow travellers, benefiting from each other at their meeting points. In a society with a strongly individualised approach to spirituality and also a strong conviction that all knowledge and experience is influenced by the interpretation of the individual, the church must do its witness with humility and openness about its own presuppositions, combined with a willingness to listen. The church will not lose face by saying, 'We do not know either, but we will explore it with you'. A genuine search is more interesting than ready-made answers. Witness happens in a dialogue.[2]

---

[1] Gabe Lyons, *The Next Christians* (Colorado Springs, CO: Multnomah, 2012), pp. 23-28. Lyons argues that the future Christian contribution will not so much be propositional and teaching certain doctrines, but rather creating community and doing initiatives that make the local community better. He argues that the future relevant Christians are the "restorers," p. 67. The book is a response to postmodern and post-Christian society and has a point worth listening to.

[2] In a lecture, Sunday 4 May 2008 in Coventry Cathedral, Yvonne Richmond, working as a priest, stated that her approach to evangelism had changed. In the 1990s she used to do evangelism with the sin-guilt-repentance-forgiveness-saved by the cross paradigm, but she learned to listen to what God was already doing in people's lives, rather than evangelising according to her own agenda. People love to share their experiences. Many have experiences with different phenomenon like angels,

Bringing a person into worship and prayer in a smaller or larger forum gives them a connection to the spiritual. Maybe the Adventist Church should consider making the experience of God a higher priority in all its services.[3] Sweeping statements are dangerous to make, but the strong emphasis in Adventism on right understanding, doctrinal positions and propositional truth at times take emphasis away from the individual experience of the transcendent and a relationship to God. The presence of the Holy Spirit cannot be manipulated, but there are ways to lead a fellowship to enter into experiences with God. The above call for neutral meetings places independent of organised religion, forums for informal, mutual and authentic conversations between trusted individuals sharing personal stories and convictions, and forums for spiritual experiences. Relationships with honesty about life and faith are settings for personal growth and meaningful development. Practical application through action makes faith and values real. These elements all seem to point in the direction of friendship, networks and smaller groups as the most relevant forums to evangelise and grow disciples today. Having said that, there are many categories of people and not all will fit into one model of ministry.

---

peace, dreams and the occult. As her main task was to interact with visitors to the Cathedral she discovered that people are spiritual although they do not take part in organised religion. Answering the question "How should we engage with people?" she recommended that we
- See others as spiritual
- Enable spiritual encounters (prayer, healing , etc)
- Explain spiritual experiences
- Nurture spiritual interest
- Journey together
- Enable relationship to God through prayer
- Relate people's experiences to what the Spirit does.

Richmond changed her teaching group to a listening group. She wanted to recognise people's experiences as genuine rather than introducing Christian idea of salvation at first. In order to reach and influence a person you have to accept them for who they are with the experiences they have, genuinely listen to them, and meet them as equals. Then mutually influence will happen.

[3] Like the experiences in the Café Church and X-preszo described in chapter 6.

A ministry model explaining the elements of a small group program will be presented in chapter 8. The rest of this chapter discusses other consequences for the Adventist Church. The traditional Adventist approach in evangelism often involved teaching new doctrines to other Christians. Some others were led to Christian faith for the first time. That was often done through a rationalistic approach, focusing on propositional truth. However, as seen in chapter 4, in the early years this approach was complemented by very strong person-to-person work carried out in people's homes by literature evangelists and Bible workers.

Evangelism has often been program-driven rather than people-oriented. Teaching has been its strongest element, often leaving out the personal, spiritual and relational. As shown in chapter 4, the employment pattern of the church has shifted dramatically. There is no longer a strong emphasis on visitation and the establishment of relationships. This has been a major weakness.

Programme-driven evangelism has had many different expressions. Public meetings have traditionally been seen as the most important method of evangelism. Over the last half century, pastors and evangelists have continued to hold public meetings as the main method for reaching out. Preparation and delivery have often taken up most of their time. Little time has been set aside for visiting potential new members of the church and results have been meagre.

Currently, the Adventist Church in Denmark has started an online outreach program called *Rejsen* [*The Journey*]."[4] It is a fine initiative and aims to reach users of the World Wide Web. Another large initiative is a private Adventist media project undertaken in Scandinavia through LifeStyleTV.[5] Both of these ministries represent heavy investment of resources in hardware and a program. Time will tell if they will be

---

[4] Seventh-Day Adventist Church Home Page, http://rejsen.net/ (accessed 2 November 2014).

[5] Seventh-Day Adventist Church Home Page, http://www.lifestyletv.se/ (accessed 2 November 2014).

able to link these media approaches as a basis for developing personal relationships. These two current examples, which seem to be worthwhile initiatives, are mentioned here to show that the Adventist Church still tends to be program-oriented. Lessons could be learned from local radio work in Scandinavia in the 1970s and 1980s. Large investments were made in technical equipment and lay people were engaged in the time-consuming work of making programs. However, the many listeners who showed interest in the Adventist faith rarely had any personal response from local churches.[6]

Research by the Lutheran National Church in Sweden in the 1990s sought to discover what existential questions people were interested in, and in what context they would like to discuss these questions. In regards to what context was good for such dialogues, 62 percent said they would like to discuss existential matters 'with one or a few of their friends' and 21 percent answered that they wanted to meet in 'a small informal group in a home', a total of 83 percent. Only 8 percent (these being women only) answered that they could see themselves discussing these issues in a church building.[7] These observations point in the direction of evangelism through relationships, networks and small groups outside formal church structures. Forums have to be

---

[6] The governments in the Scandinavian countries loosened up the state monopoly on radio in the 1970s and allowed local organisations to establish themselves on new channels. Many local churches saw this as an opportunity to reach a large number of people with the gospel. A large financial outlay was involved and pastors and lay people invested long hours in this ministry. Little was achieved, however, in terms of conversions, discipleship or church growth. To my knowledge, no significant research has been conducted on this wave in evangelism. My personal observation, from having talked with many of those involved, is that so much energy went into the programme (investment in equipment, logistics, the preparation of programmes and delivery on air), that no time was left for personal work. In 2002, the local radio station at the Stockholm Adventist Church had three-thousand cards with contact information for people who had communicated with the station, but, strangely, no time was set aside for visits or follow-up. This represents an approach to evangelism that focuses on running a programme.

[7] Rolf Gustafson, *Tid För Dialog* [Time for Dialogue] (Uppsala: Trotts Allt, 1994), p. 37.

established where there is an atmosphere of trust, liberty for all to express themselves, respect for anyone's opinion, a sense of equality and commitment to the small group. This research from Sweden corresponds to the more recent experiences from the Café Church and X-preszo in their small groups and Matthew-parties.

In view of the changes in culture that are demonstrated in this study, the Adventist Church needs to carry out its evangelism in the context of relationships. This will call for a less professional ministries run by pastors and leaders, and a much more significant contribution will be needed from the lay people of the church, something which probably would benefit all.[8] The new situation demands from pastors a somewhat different set of skills. This eventually affects the curriculum and methods of theological education, something I, in my current role, must give serious consideration.

The individualistic mentality challenges the traditional programs of the church and to some degree the existence of the central organisation. The individualist, who considers himself or herself to be the reference point, does not come to a community only to listen, but also to be heard and to test out ideas with others. No one is seen to have more authority than another. This leads to a clash of cultures as the programs in the church most often are designed to promote the ideas of the institution.

Worship services invite participation in singing and praying, but do not open the door for an exchange of ideas. The one-way communication of the sermon is not used in many other forums in the Danish society. In news-services, talk shows and even classrooms, people look at various points of view, and each person is encouraged to form a personal opinion. The church needs to think hard about what forum it will create for discussions that are open-ended. Most Adventist churches have a Bible study hour before the "divine

---

[8] Russell Burrill, *Revolution in the Church* (Fallbrook, CA: Hart Research Center, 1993), .among others, have called for the unleashing of the lay people in the Adventist Church.

service" every Saturday (Sabbath school). This is potentially a very good opportunity for dialogue. However, the traditional Bible study guides seem rigid to a questioning mind. The study guides are usually designed with questions, followed by one or two Bible passages and an explanatory paragraph which gives the answer to the questions. This style does not encourage independent thinking and is far different from the teaching methods used in school classrooms or in universities.

Even public church meetings have generally followed the model of monologues and the delivery of information. Several local churches have started to use materials that allow for open-ended discussions. People want a dialogue that gives all parties equal standing and input. The popularity of blogs, phone-in programmes and the like demonstrate the importance of a two-way exchange and the democratisation of ideas in today's world. This spills over to issues of spirituality.

The Adventist Church does not necessarily have to change its doctrines to develop a different profile,[9] but it needs to state its *raison d'être* in a life-affirming way,[10] helping people to discover meaning for

---

[9] George Knight, an Adventist historian quoted throughout chapter 5, discusses this in *The Neutering of Adventism*. George R Knight, *The Apocalyptic Vision and the Neutering of Adventism* (Hagerstown, MD: Review & Herald, 2008). His first argument is that the Adventist Church needs to have a stronger focus on Christ and the gospel of grace. But he also states that if the Adventist Church forgets its particular doctrines and its prophetic message, it will lose its identity and thereby its reason for existence. That is probably true if one is speaking about a Christian society, but in relation to a spiritual seeker in Danish society the church will probably find its strength in providing meaning, resources for spiritual growth and worthwhile principles and values to live by. The church still will be able to maintain its doctrines, but that will not be the main focus in its initial contact with seekers.

[10] The present world leadership puts a lot of emphasis on the Adventist particular doctrines which were formulated in the 1800s. That has its place, but these formulations do not necessarily speak to the needs of the Northern European. The emphasis on doctrines has been strong in many public presentations and been transmitted widely. Two examples would be the first sermon of the world leader after his election (http://www.youtube.

their lives, find spiritual values and provide them with opportunities to put these into practice in real relationships. The church would profit from considering how it can provide room for individuals to find their own paths forward. Many are looking for a framework of thought, values and lifestyle that gives guidance to their lives. The Adventist Church can provide such a framework, but it is better presented as an offer than a straight-jacket.

If the building blocks of the Adventist Church were small groups rather than local churches, that would call for a more relational philosophy of ministry, a different model for pastoral work, a heavier reliance on the lay people of the church, a slightly different approach to membership (as discussed above), and new bonds to tie the church together. That would constitute a ministry revolution, and in my opinion that is needed. Revolution usually involves conflict, pain and bloodshed and it is unlikely to come from central leadership. Still if the leadership see the need, they can let, and even inspire, individuals to try out new methods in church plants and pilot projects. These elements will be expanded on in chapter 8, which analyse how small groups can have a central function in the Adventist organisation. Unconventional models have been tried and proven helpful elsewhere and at other times.[11]

Making small groups the main forum for individual growth, teaching and discipleship does not necessarily mean that other church programs will be redundant. Periodic worship in a larger group will still have meaning, but the purpose of these gatherings will probably be different. Worship will be highly spiritual providing the

---

com/playlist?list=PLB72DA3F3193CCC16) and his speech at the annual council in 2010 (http://www.youtube.com/watch?v=NqxzN8rdSC8). The church needs to bring forward some of its more practical contributions to personal life and the community, how it can help each individual on their journey through life, and the spiritual aspects of the Christian walk.

[11] Three European churches were mentioned in chapter 6. A local church in Auckland, New Zealand, drops the Sabbath Morning service every second week in order to meet in homes and do community work. Kent Kingston, 'A Fresh Vision of Church', *Adventist Record*, (5 April 2014), 14–15.

visitors opportunities to worship through song, communal prayers, intercessory prayers, meditative readings and personal reflections. Less emphasis will be put on the teaching element of the sermon since this will happen in the groups.

Gatherings in the larger group, church, might not happen every week, as the main church event is the small group. Such a model will be different from a traditional church model and many members will find it strange and unfulfilling. Even more threatening might be the idea that some church buildings might not be needed any more. Such a thought is highly controversial and actually acting on it can lead to painful conflict. Pilot projects and isolated trial ministries might be a way forward.

Growth and discipleship happen in relationships under the guidance of the Holy Spirit. It is not a cleverly designed program, strategic advertising, the best speaker or wonderful facilities that bring it about. It is when individuals live in relationships with real people, honestly sharing life's struggles, and where prayer, Bible study and personal reflection is done in an authentic way, that people are gradually formed. They need to be given space, be accepted as they are and share the challenge it is to be under the influence of the Holy Spirit and the Word of God. Individualism is challenged under the guidance of the Spirit. As CK said above: praying and reading the Bible created 'the question in their own mind as to whether they are the central shaft around which the universe is turning. . . People meet God in prayer'.

The conclusions presented here might seem simple and of little consequence. Nothing could be further from the truth. If such a new mind-set is allowed to dictate the church's operation it will, as shown, have serious consequences for most aspects of church life: teaching, evangelism, membership, buildings, pastoral training, role of laity, use of finances and much more. Changes will happen and leadership will have the choice of either just letting things evolve randomly and inefficiently or taking a commanding role, intentionally leading the church according to a vision and a plan.

There have been many theological discussions and the Adventist Church has matured. The multiplicity of peoples, cultures and ideas among its eighteen-million members has opened up the denomination to more flexibility. The European situation is unique in the world church. Few outside European Adventism understand it. Hopefully church leaders and members will take lessons from the biblical examples of change, as well as from the church's current experience of differences as exemplified in chapter 6, and support a new approach in Europe conducting a ministry that has an emphasis that meets the current culture.

To find ways to reach the Danish people has importance for the church in Europe and wider Western World as well as the rapidly urbanising and secularised parts of the developing world. It is not unlikely that the changes that are taking place in Western Europe today will also become a reality in other parts of the world in the near future.[12] That is still a matter for conjecture, but if the church can find a way to make disciples for Christ in the Northern European environment today, that experience may profit the global Church in the future. The final chapter will elaborate further on possible solutions and draw conclusions for practical ministry.

---

[12] There are also indications to the contrary. Davie argues that Europe is the 'exceptional case' and that belief in the supernatural will remain strong on other continents. Davie, *Europe*, x.

CHAPTER 8

Small group ministry in the Adventist context

The conclusions in the previous chapter made clear that the formation of caring relationships, small groups and networks are increasingly important in the mission of the church. In the Danish context evangelism would best take place in a neutral venue outside the church building, often in small groups of people. This is not a dogmatic approach as if there was one answer to all situations. The use of networks and small groups can go hand-in-hand with many forms of evangelism, and in the current Danish population they will prove significant. This chapter provides a rationale from the early church and early Adventist history for the importance of small groups.[1] Furthermore it suggests a leadership model for a change in church culture to move the whole organisation towards a more organic and relational understanding of the church and its mission. Since a wealth of material has been published on and for small groups, creating yet another program may not be the most important contribution to make. Therefore, only a short summary of some key elements for the running of small groups follows below.

---

1 "Small Groups" is here used as a common expression for informal meetings with up to approximately a dozen people. Different terminologies are used in literature: house groups, life groups, cell groups, units and more. The emphasis here is on a forum for the personal, authentic and relational elements in Christian fellowship.

Biblical Basis for Small Groups

Most scholars conclude that for the first two-hundred years of the church's history there were hardly any purpose-built churches; believers met in private houses. The strong growth that Christianity experienced during the first two centuries took place in house churches.[2] The majority of Christians were poorer people who would not own or rent properties where significant numbers of people could meet. According to archaeological discoveries most people in the Middle East lived in very humble dwellings with limited space, being tenements with a workplace on the ground floor and living quarters in two or three floors above. This would limit the number of people who could meet at one time.[3] Wealthier families had buildings or apartments made up of several rooms to accommodate extended families, with more than two generations of family members and their slaves living in each household.[4] To have one large room where thirty-to-fifty people could gather was a privilege of the rich.[5]

---

[2] Edin Løvås, *Husmenigheten (The House Church)* (Kvinesdal: Hermon Forlag, 1984), p. 16.

[3] Bradley S. Billings, 'From House Church to Tenement Church', *Journal of Theological Studies*, 62:2 (2011), 541–69.

[4] Robert J. Banks, *Paul's Idea of Community: The Early House Churches in Their Historical Setting* (Grand Rapids, MI: Eerdmans, 1980), p. 41.

[5] There are several examples of this practice described in the Acts of the Apostles. Thousands of people became Christians in Jerusalem and Judea in the first years after the resurrection of Jesus (2.41; 4.4). They did not have formal meeting places but met regularly in the temple and in homes for fellowship, prayer and meals (2.43-47). There is a reference to a group of Christians meeting in the house of 'Mary the mother of John, also called Mark' (12.12). At Philippi, Paul met Lydia, who became a Christian. The Christians used her house as a meeting place (16.14-15). In Corinth Paul started teaching in the synagogue, but met with considerable opposition. He then began teaching in the home of Titius Justus (18.7). It is recorded that in Troas, on one occasion, Paul taught far into the night. This episode seems to have occurred in a private home (20.7-12). The epistles make several references to local churches meeting in the houses of large families. Writing to the church in Corinth, Paul sends greetings from Priscilla and Aquinas and 'the church that meets at their house' (1 Cor 16.19). In the letter to the Colossians, Paul asks them to 'Give my greetings to the brothers at Laodicea, and to Nympha and the church in her house' (Col

The simple fact that the early church met in private homes may have been the result of necessity more than of conviction. The Christian movement was often an underground organisation and its members did not have the rights or the finances to build their own official buildings. The fact that the church met in homes back then is not an argument for it to do the same today. However, there are elements in the meaning and purpose of Christian fellowship that point convincingly in the direction of an informal gathering of people. The early Christians were sharing, caring, praying, eating and teaching as they met. The church was meant to provide an alternative type of fellowship; an environment in which the principles of the kingdom were lived. The church was a community where people grew as disciples of Jesus.

In their book *Building a Church of Small Groups*,[6] Bill Donahue and Russ Robinson list some of the theological and sociological arguments for the small group as an important aspect of Christian life. First, they state that, 'Since God himself lives and works in [a] community and since we are created in God's image, then we are created in and for community'.[7] Second, this community is relational, as is also shown in the life of Jesus.[8] Third, they refer to "oneness," as found in John 17, in which the oneness of the three persons in the Godhead is mentioned and an invitation is given to people to be one with them and one with each other.[9] Donahue and Robinson go on to describe qualities such as dependence, interdependence, the strength and wisdom in a fellowship, accountability and acceptance as factors that speak for the need to have small groups.

    4.15). Again, in the letter to Philemon, Paul wishes grace and peace to him and "to the church that meets in your home" (Phil 2).

[6] Bill Donahue and Russ Robinson, *Building a Church of Small Groups: A Place Where Nobody Stands Alone* (Grand Rapids, MI: Zondervan, 2001). See also Phil Potter, *The Challenge of Cell Church: Getting to Grips with Cell Church Values* (Oxford: Bible Reading Fellowship, 2001). See, in particular, chapters 4 and 5 (pp. 63-93), on discipleship and community.

[7] Ibid., p. 23.
[8] Ibid., p. 26.
[9] Ibid., p. 29.

They also point to the biblical picture of the church as one body, with Christ as its head (1 Cor 12; Eph 4). That metaphor calls for close relationships and a sharing of life.[10] Robert Banks, in *Paul's Idea of Community*, adds to this theological basis for small groups. He writes about the metaphor of the body and notes the close relationship of Christians to Christ and to each other: 'Each member of the community is granted a ministry to other members of the community. . . . So close is the link between members of the community that what affects one necessarily affects all'.[11] Banks notes that Paul uses the language of household and family life to describe relationships in the church.[12] Paul wrote to the Corinthians about his love for them (1 Cor 16.24; 4.21; 10.14): 'He clearly expected Christians in their various local churches to enter into the same kinds of loving relationships with one another'.[13] The church, whether large or small, should be organised in such a way that these relationships can be formed and strengthened.

Another biblical goal for the church is to support personal discipleship development. This cannot happen in a big crowd but can take place in the context of close relationships with care and trust. Some of these values and functions are brought forward in Gareth Icenogle's *Biblical Foundations for Small Group Ministry* particularly in chapters 19 and 20. He shows how the small group can be transformational. It is a healing community, a place for recognising, confessing and

---

[10] Ibid., pp. 33–52.
[11] Banks, *Paul's Idea of Community*, pp. 63-64.
[12] Ibid., pp. 54–61. This is true of the bond between Jesus and the Father and also for the church members' relationship to God and each other. Such terms include "my child," "beloved brother," "father," "our brother," "our sister," "his mother and mine," "household of faith," "household of God" and the Greek term *oikeioi* (a family term used to describe the Christian community). Banks notes that many of Paul's expressions, particularly in the closing words of his letters, 'witness to the strong 'family' character of the relationships built up by Paul and various members of the churches amongst whom he moved,' p. 56.
[13] Ibid., p. 57.

forgiving sin. It is a place of personal and group prayer. It is a healing agent in the world, a community of love turned in to practice.[14]

The house meetings of the New Testament church took on many forms, according to need. Kurt Johnson notes that the book of Acts describes several types of house meeting.[15] Today there are many ways in which small groups can be used to build up Christian fellowship. These descriptions of what the church should contribute to Christian life leave a strong message. Many Christians, as they meet in large gatherings in traditional churches for a one-hour, weekly worship service, do not experience a fraction of what church fellowship should be like or what it could do for them. It is small fellowship and the close community that can provide this biblical reality for believers.

Small Groups in the Adventist Church

The Adventist Church started as a network of small communities which met in private homes throughout the North-eastern states of the US, and could well be classified as a small-group movement. Things have changed radically and the church has copied the practices of the traditional church from the middle Ages where the main service was where the lay people stood and the professional ministers operate up front. In many local Danish churches Adventists meet in groups of twenty-to-forty people weekly. These small communities could implement some of the mechanisms of the small group if they were not so tied to a certain tradition for how church services should be conducted.

---

[14] Gareth Weldon Icenogle, *Biblical Foundations for Small Group Ministry* (Downers Grove, IL: InterVarsity Press, 1993), pp. 295–303.

[15] Kurt W Johnson, *Small Groups for the End Time: A Practical Guide for the Twenty-first Century* (Hagerstown, MD: Review & Herald, 1997), p. 53. Prayer meeting (12.12), evening of Christian fellowship (21.7), common meals, possibly communion services (2.46), a night of prayer, worship and instruction (20.7), impromptu evangelistic gatherings (16.32), meetings planned for the presentation of the gospel (10.22), following up of those inquiring about the gospel (18.26) and meetings for organisational instruction (5.42).

In chapter 4 reference was made to Sabbath school, the weekly Bible study, and its roots in Methodism and Wesley's class meetings.[16] As noted, Sabbath school has gradually changed over time. From being a time when one discussed the Bible, prayed for each other and planned service for the community and evangelism, the Sabbath school has increasingly become a Bible study forum.[17] Thus the Adventist Church has lost from its program a key forum for care, fellowship, discipleship and evangelism. It is my opinion, in light of the research supporting this study, that the revival of a small- group ministry in the Adventist Church is vital for the denomination's survival. This thinking seems to correspond to the ideas of the early Adventists. Ellen White, a key thinker and leader in the early Adventist Church, wrote of small groups (not specifically of Sabbath school classes) in 1902: 'The formation of small companies as a basis of Christian effort has been presented to me by One who cannot err. If there is a large number in the church, let the members be formed into small companies, to work not only for the church members, but for unbelievers'.[18] Ellen White also saw the importance of relationships in evangelism, as is illustrated in this quotation dating from 1905: 'Christ's method alone will give true success in reaching the people. The Saviour mingled with men as one who desired their good. He showed His sympathy for them, ministered to their needs, and won their confidence. Then He bade them, "Follow Me"'.[19]

---

[16] See chapter 4 for details. Some of the founders of Adventism had roots in the Methodist Church and there is a link between their practice and what was later established as Sabbath school.

[17] D. Michael Henderson, *A Model for Making Disciples: John Wesley's Class Meeting* (Evangel Publishing House, 2005), p. 83. Wesley established groups for several different needs. There were five different types of groups: The society, the class meeting, the band, the select society and the penitent bands, pp. 83-126. The Sabbath school in Adventist cycles have been turned into what Wesley would call 'the Society.'

[18] Ellen G. White, *Testimonies for the Church*, Vol. 6 (Mountain View, CA: Pacific Press, 1948), pp. 21-22.

[19] White, *The Ministry of Healing*, 143.

There were several types of small groups in operation in the early days of the history of the Adventist Church.[20] For a time small groups in the form of Sabbath schools worked as a church-planting program. A few members from an established church would set up a field Sabbath school in a neighbouring community, invite friends and through that small group ministry gradually build a new church. This practice has dwindled. There was a particular emphasis on small groups in the 1990s in the Adventist Church, reflecting a similar priority in Christianity at large.[21] Sabbath school, with its more theoretical discussions, has continued as a practice in traditional Adventist Churches but small groups, in the sense of house meetings held at times of the week other than Saturday (Sabbath) mornings are

[20] Johnson, *Small Groups for the End Time*. Chapter 7 of this volume gives a more detailed description of the link, through Ellen White, between the Methodist class meeting and the Adventist Church's small group practices. It also lists several types of house meetings favoured by the Adventist Church in the early days, within a list of Adventist meetings in general. These included Cottage Meeting, Bible Readings, the Social Meeting [connected to church services], Sabbath School, Personal visitation and Bible Study. All would have included some of the elements of 'prayer, testimonies, word of encouragement to each other, singing and fellowship,' pp. 64-68.

[21] Some of the publications which were part of the emphasis on small groups in the Adventist Church in the 1990s should be noted here, starting with Calvin L. Smith, *Church Growth through Sabbath School Action Units* (Department of Church Ministries, General Conference of Adventist Church, 1992). Kurt W Johnson, who at that time was the personal ministries and Sabbath school director for the Oregon Conference of Seventh-day Adventists, published two books on small groups which were widely circulated: *Small Group Outreach: How to Begin and Lead Outreach Bible Study Groups* (Hagerstown, MD: Review & Herald, 1991) and *Small Groups for the End Time;* W. Clarence Schilt, *Dynamic Small Groups: How to Make Them Happen* (Hagerstown, MD: Review & Herald, 1992); Curtis Rittenour, *Coming Together: Experiencing God through Scripture* (Lincoln, NE: Centre for Creative Ministry, Advent Source, 1998); David Cox, *Think Big, Think Small Groups* (Watford: Department of Personal Ministries, Adventist Church, 1998). This volume came out after a strong emphasis had been given to small groups in teaching seminars throughout the Trans-European Division of the Adventist Church. Martin Vukmanic, *Så Startar Du En Smågrupp* [*How to Start a Small Group*] (Stockholm: Adventistsamfundet [The Adentist Church], 1995). This material was part of a teaching emphasis on small-group ministries in the local churches.

rare. Sabbath school and the traditional midweek meetings have the potential to reignite the sense of fellowship and spiritual community. However, small groups have been used as strong evangelistic tools in several church plants over recent years, as illustrated by the two case studies presented in chapter 6.

Small Group Ministry in the Current Culture

Leaders of the church plants mentioned in chapter 6, emphasised the importance of small groups (in their terminology, "cell groups" or "life groups") in establishing new churches. They saw small-group ministry as a strong discipling tool, offering a relevant forum for people to come and talk about their experience of God and nurture personal faith. In this study the function of small groups as a connecting element between the church and society is emphasised. There is however a wide spectrum of ministries and spiritual fellowships that work well within the context of a small group.[22] The following is an examination of elements that need to be present in a small group. This is discussed with reference to the analysis of the Danish population in chapters 2, 3 and 7.

Individualism might be the single strongest factor that has changed in the mentality of the Danish population. People, particularly the younger generations, use themselves as reference points for what they believe and how they want to grow. The small group can make provision for individuals to develop faith on their own terms, if the group is willing to give each member the space they need. It is in an

---

[22] Small groups function best when they have a specific purpose. The purpose can be achieved within the group itself or as a ministry for some outside the group. Often the group meetings are more profitable and sustainable if people gather around a common cause. Meetings can have the purpose of exploring existential questions, faith and lifestyle, or practical life issues like how to be a parent or how to have a good marriage. Doing a ministry for the community is another option for the group. That can take on multiple forms. Accountability groups, Bible study groups, discipleship groups . . . The strength of all forms of groups are that they create small, safe and hopefully authentic fellowships where people can be themselves and grow.

environment where any statements or reflections are welcomed and accepted as being genuine, and where each person will find space and time to develop viewpoints and opinions on his or her own terms. For many, the mere circumstance of relating to existential questions more deeply than before and of approaching the divine and spiritual is a new and strange exercise. Garry Poole points this out in *Seeker Small Groups*. He writes: 'Most seekers have never fully considered what they believe and why they believe it. But once those starting points [love, mutual respect, and authenticity] are established, the leader can formulate a series of questions that require the group members to move logically from one point of understanding to another in their thinking about God and their relationship with him'.[23] People want to find their own truth. It can be similar to the beliefs others hold, but it must be genuinely their own.

It was observed earlier that Danes in general are apt to pick and combine religious beliefs according to their own taste as they use themselves as the ultimate reference point.[24] This brings a tension when they enter a group which uses the Bible as an authority and a reference point. The two will argue from different platforms. As the members of the Café Church pointed out in their interview, a basic premise of their small group is that it involves prayer and reference to the Bible. That practice is not used in an authoritative and manipulative way, but members of the small group are introduced to the thoughts and teachings of the Bible and are influenced by prayer and by the Holy Spirit. That opens people's minds, so that they

---

[23] Garry Poole, *Seeker Small Groups: Engaging Spiritual Seekers in Life-changing Discussions* (Grand Rapids, MI: Zondervan: Willow Creek Resources, 2003), p. 121.

[24] She describes the mix of religion with a reference to 'the many individuals who feel inspired by Asian religions when it comes to reincarnation, yoga, meditation, and personal development. These are examples of an individual patchwork religion and spirituality that we [*the Danish Pluralism Project*] believe can give an indication as to how religion is changing in Denmark.' The dogmatic approach of organised religion is on the retreat and an individually defined spirituality is on the rise. Marianne C. Qvortrup Fibiger, 'The Danish Pluralism Project', *Religion*, 39:2 (2009), 175.

reconsider biblical ideas.[25] It is necessary for the group to give all the members room to develop ownership of their own faith and thinking.

A further characteristic of Danes in general is that they are more spiritual than religious. This means that people tend to "believe in something" (which they often cannot define) rather than holding on to a traditional set of Christian dogmas about God or maintaining a particular religious viewpoint. God is seen as a special spiritual power rather than the personal God described in the Bible. Christian small groups will necessarily hold on to biblical ideas and refer to its Christian theories and traditions. It is still possible for a group to meet the spiritual search among Danes. A group can emphasise the spiritual aspects of the Christian experience. The topics discussed by the members can be highly relevant to people's life situations, and can bring helpful contributions to the questions and issues people struggle with. Interviewees from both the Café Church[26] and X-preszo[27] mentioned the spiritual interest people had.

They experienced, through their services and small groups, that people wanted the "real thing" – faith in the supernatural and how to approach and understand God. The small group should be openly spiritual. The experience of the interviewed church leaders shows that it was exactly the spiritual element that attracted visitors' interest. The small group should try to connect its members to the divine and to God. This conclusion is in harmony with the research referred to in the foregoing chapters.

The issues of belonging and socialisation are also strong elements in the small group. Most people want to be part of a fellowship where they are accepted exactly as they are. Society has changed dramatically and people tend to live disconnected from their extended families, locally-based societies and other traditional groups. Those traditional

---

[25] Susanne Kalvaag and Cyril Kalvaag, The Café Church - 1, Skype Interview, 19 August 2013.
[26] Ibid.
[27] Martin Altink et al., X-preszo, Focus Group, 25 August 2013.

structures used to be the carriers of common beliefs, faith and values. Society as a whole is now inclined to be more secular and the structures that kept people in a faith system have been lost. The small group seems to provide a clear alternative community that helps people define and keep their faith. As shown in chapter 2 the group to which a person belongs will influence the content and structure of that individual's faith. The interaction in the group will lead its members in a similar direction and as the Bible is used as an important reference point, the members will be moved in the direction of biblical spirituality and faith.

The relationship between membership of a small group and a person's relationship to a larger church body also deserves some consideration. A strong relationship to a small group does not necessarily bring about a link or commitment to a larger church organisation or denomination. A small-group ministry that is set up by a local church, which belongs to a particular denomination, may have a strategy to guide members of associated groups towards the particular thinking, lifestyle and understanding of the denomination. However, this has to happen within the context of respect, openness and flexibility. In view of current changes in society and culture, it is more likely that new believers place their loyalty where their relationships are.

The Adventist Church, along with other churches in Denmark, should seriously rethink its *modus operandi* and allow for a network of smaller groups to be the forum for those interested in their spiritual formation. In such a setting, membership is no longer the main focus of evangelism but rather to help people towards faith and a meaningful life. It is not unlikely that an organisation that focuses less on membership and more on spiritual values will end up having more members. Having a more open community goes against Adventist traditional thinking where growth of the institution carried much significance.

If the meeting in the small group becomes more important than the traditional church service, that new thinking must be reflected in the church organisation. A practical solution can be to have weekly meetings in small groups and only meet bi-weekly or monthly for a larger gathering. If teaching happens in the small groups, the larger services might change in form and be an opportunity for worship more than listening to proclamation. Having a different structure, might pose a threat to the establishment. From an administrative point of view, questions of membership, tithing and loyalty to the organisation immediately come to mind. The church should ask itself the question however, what model will be most useful in helping more Danes be followers of Jesus Christ. Some of these organisational questions will be wrestled with by leaders elsewhere. Fears of a Trojan horse will appear. The purpose of this paper is to present a model which corresponds to the present reality.

Establishing a Small Group Ministry

As described in chapter 4, the Adventist Church tends to be hierarchical in its structure, program oriented in its evangelism and propositional in its presentation of the gospel. All these are obstacles in Danish culture. Changes have to happen on all levels, but as the ministry of the church happens in local churches, that is the most important place for change. A move towards a small group emphasis will call for looser structures, more organic and relational evangelism and a more existential presentation of Adventism.

This represents a major shift towards a present-day paradigm, but not necessarily a rejection of the past. Such a shift calls for brave leadership both centrally and in each local church, and careful thought needs to go into the presentations of new values and attitudes and eventually the establishment of new practices and behaviours in the whole organisation. The following the eight step theory of change presented by John Kotter of Harvard Business School, in *Leading*

Change[28] and *The Heart of Change*[29] will be used as a guide for a process of change in the Adventist Church.

The first step in Kotter's process is to Increase Urgency. Except for the last few years the Adventist Church in Denmark has seen decline for half-a-century. Stagnation and the constant pain of a slowly diminishing membership have become normal. If the church is not fulfilling the task of making disciples, given by Christ, it is in crisis. Leadership has to be truthful and express dissatisfaction with the status quo. The sense of urgency must be accompanied by a rational and analytical understanding of the situation.

That will include the involvement of all levels of leaders and members in an honest analysis of where the church stands in its ministry in its present context. Knowledge and analysis of current culture and traits, similar to those presented in this study need to be taught to pastors and members. The urgency is not whether the church has small groups or not; it is related to whether it fulfils its mission. The emphasis on the personal and relational comes as part of a vision. Bill Hybels, senior pastor of Willow Creek Community Church and key speaker and organiser of the Global Leadership Summits,[30] increasingly emphasises that to lead a church to take up a challenge for change there is not only a need to explain where to go but 'why we cannot stay here'.[31]

The second principle is to build the guiding team. Whether this process should come as the first step before increasing the urgency can be discussed. For the leadership in the Danish Adventist Church it is crucial to find support in key leaders; both formal and informal.

---

[28] John P. Kotter, *Leading Change* (Boston: Harvard Business Review Press, 2012).
[29] Ibid.
[30] Willow Creek, 'Leadership', WillowCreek.com, http://www.willowcreek.com/ events/leadership/ (accessed 2 November 2014).
[31] Bill Hybels, 'From Here to There' (Lecture presented at the Global Leadership Summit, DVD, Willow Creek Community Church: Willow Creek Association UK and Ireland, 2010).

As Kotter expands on in *A Force for Change*, effective leadership is a team effort[32] and scholars agree that in the New Testament church leadership was always done by teams.[33] Introducing new values and new methods will inspire the entrepreneurs, the creative and imaginative members of the church, who often are frustrated when the church remains in a state of status quo.

This group can be compared to the apostles and prophets of the early church who took the church to new places—both geographically and in its ministry.[34] These kinds of people will be the strong supporters of change. It is wise to limit the change process to a pilot project involving pastors and elders of churches (church plants) which are open for new models of ministry. That would also open for the early wins described below. The testimonies of the interviewed leaders prove that these kind of leaders can be found and that pilot projects can take off and thrive in the Adventist community.

Kotter's third principle is to get the vision right. A vision is a picture of a preferred future. It is a description of how things could be and creates enthusiasm about getting there. The leadership team must know where they want to go and why before they present a vision. In the Adventist Church a vision of a more relational and existential approach to Christianity must be carried by a thorough teaching and implication of a different value system. This is not done overnight or in a couple of sermons at a camp meeting. There must be a strategic plan of how to change values over a period of time.

---

[32] Kotter, *A Force for Change*, pp. 77–88.
[33] Harper, *Let My People Grow*, 174–176. See also Frost and Hirsch, *The Shaping of Things to Come*, pp. 169–173.
[34] Frost, Hirsch, Alan, *The Shaping of Things to Come*, pp. 182–191. Frost and Hirsch discuss the APEPT model (Apostle, prophet, evangelist, pastor and teacher) as found in Eph 4.11 and notice that new churches and organisations are intensive on the leadership aspects of apostles, prophets and evangelists whereas established churches tend to rely on teachers and pastors.

Although a few are very receptive to new ideas, the majority of church members are slow to accept change. It is only as new values are integrated with the receivers that new practices will be accepted. This process is outlined in Robert Lewis and Wayne Cordeiro's volume *Culture Shift*. They argue that the leader of a local church must first understand the present value system of his/her church. Then a work of introducing more biblical and Christian values can begin. This must be a conscious process using several media. New values are not established when they are proclaimed, but rather when they have been established in new programs, practices and behaviours that stay.[35]

The forth step is communicate for buy-in. John Maxwell writes, 'Leadership is influence – nothing more, nothing less'.[36] Change in a church setting comes through influence – not through manipulation, force or gullible optimism. The Christian leader will, together with his/her team, use various means to help all members understand new values, attitudes and corresponding ministry models, and how these relate to God's will. The obvious methods often seem to be preaching and teaching, but in no other context is influence as strong as in the one-to-one conversation. Change can best be brought about through a strong visitation program where leaders meet individuals in their homes, at lunch-breaks, in cafés, walking in parks or any other setting. To get a conversation going in the whole organisation is optimal. The leader of a volunteer organisation does not have the same power as a leader in an organisation where the members are paid to do a task. Influence is all that he/she has.[37]

Empower Action, step five, means removing obstacles and setting people free to act.[38] Removing obstacles will include taking away old

---

[35] Robert Lewis, Wayne Cordeiro and Warren Bird, *Culture Shift: Transforming Your Church from the Inside Out* (San Francisco: John Wiley & Sons, 2005), pp. 53–67.
[36] John C. Maxwell, *The 21 Irrefutable Laws of Leadership* (Nashville, TN: Thomas Nelson, 1998), p. 17.
[37] Ibid., p. 18.
[38] Kotter, *The Heart of Change*, pp. 103–104, 123.

baggage in the form of prejudices and overly cautious arguments holding on to the past. Sometimes even people who are totally resistant to change need to be removed from leadership or even the fellowship. For Kotter, who writes for a secular context, empowering includes: 'Finding individuals with change experience who can bolster people's self-confidence with the we-won-you-can-too [sic] anecdotes. Recognition and reward systems that inspire, promote optimism, and build self-confidence. Feedback that can help people make better vision-related decisions. 'Re-tooling' disempowering managers by giving them new jobs that clearly show the need for change'.[39] Adjustments of these points to a church setting can be done. For example would conflict resolution for old conflicts, be an area that could need attention.

The sixth step, Create Short-term wins, was alluded to above. Members need encouragement and the best of sort is real life results. That is a challenge in the current spiritual climate in Denmark where evangelism is hard. A similar outcome can be achieved by excursions to see churches where new methods have worked, visit conferences where testimonies are made, provide literature with real case studies and have visiting speakers bearing witness to how new ministry form give results.

Don't let up and Make change stick are the two last steps which are of similar character. Kotter declares that it is important not to be 'declaring victory prematurely'.[40] This often happens in church. Pastors and other leaders tend to believe that after some sermons and/ or a teaching seminar on the issues, which find a good response in members, that change is more or less settled. Often, nothing could be further from the truth. Leaders must remember that conclusions they have reached after months of studies, prayer and discussions will not be accepted by their members in a matter of hours or days. On top of a prolonged period promoting a philosophy of ministry,

---

[39] Ibid., p. 123.
[40] Ibid., p. 143.

change has to be put into new routines and behaviours. Only when such has been established for a while, has change really happened.[41] People tend to remember the past and "the good old days" seem sweeter as the challenges of new ways arrive. Therefore there needs to be a constant repetition of the vision and its corresponding values, teaching, coaching and monitoring until the organisation operates in a new way. Hybels, in his final part of the keynote address at the Global Leadership Summit 2013, emphasised the importance of going beyond the vision and actually establishing a system and routines for it so that it will stay.[42] The benefits of the new ways must be celebrated.

If small groups in a local church shall fulfil their purpose of making disciples a structure of leaders must be established. This has been described and analysed extensively in other literature, so a brief summary is sufficient here. Each group should have committed leaders[43] who are trained and mentored.[44] The small group leaders need to be part of leader fellowships for training,[45] strategic thinking and for keeping the common vision alive throughout the network of small groups.[46] Only an intentional use of the small groups will keep the whole structure focused on its purpose. Neal McBride writes, 'Managing the small-groups ministry is best accomplished by design rather than by default'.[47] There is a balance between flexibility

---

[41] Ibid., p. 176.
[42] Hybels, ‚The Courage Leadership Requires'.
[43] John Mallison, *Small Group Leader: A Manual to Develop Vital Small Groups* (Bletchley: Scripture Union Publishing, 1996), pp. 44–54.
[44] Dale Galloway, *The Small Group Book* (Grand Rapids, MI: Revell, 1995), pp. 89–110.
[45] Thomas G. Kirkpatrick, *Small Groups in the Church: A Handbook for Creating Community* (Bethesda, MD: Alban Institute, 1995), pp. 45–86. This section includes detailed suggestions on how leadership training can be planned.
[46] Donahue, *Building a Church of Small Groups*, pp. 145–156, 177–193.
[47] Neal McBride, *How to Build a Small Groups Ministry* (Colorado Springs, CO: NavPress, 1995), p. 155. This volume outlines practical mechanisms for leading and administering a network of small groups.

and individual needs on the one hand and an overall strategy from the church leadership on the other. In such a model of monitoring, accountability and mentoring a multiplicity of small groups can operate within the framework of an overall local church strategy. It is advisable that the small group ministry is led by a designated coordinator, which could be the pastor.[48]

Leading a Small Group

There are many different needs that can be met by a small group. According to the types of people taking part, emphasis can be given to different needs.[49] Most of the literature that offers guidance on organising small groups lists four or five basic elements which should be in place in a meeting: sharing and caring, praying for each other, studying and learning, a ministry for others and food. There is a wealth of literature[50] on the practical aspects of running a small group, so the details of the small group meeting will not be covered in

---

[48] Mallison, *Small Group Leader*, p. 48.
[49] Donahue and Robinson put groups into categories according to age/stage (couples, singles, men, women, children, youth), task (volunteer ministry), interest (investigating faith or other subject), and care (AA, ACOA, grief recovery, divorce recovery), p. 211. In *Making Small Groups Work*, Cloud and Townsend introduce four types of groups: Bible/book study (studying the Bible or books about the Bible), topical support group (on marriage, parenting, dating, relationships), recovery (addictions, bad habits, divorce), and general support groups (spiritual, emotional, and personal growth), p. 123. In *The Big Book on Small Groups*, Jeffrey Arnold divides groups into five categories: cell groups, discipleship groups, ministry groups, special-needs groups, affinity groups and house-churches, pp. 76-81.
[50] Publications on the subject include the following: Cloud and Townsend, *Making Small Groups Work*; David Cox, *Think Big, Think Small Groups*. Donahue, *Building a Church of Small Groups*; Donahue, *Leading Life-changing Small Groups*; Johnson, *Small Group Outreach*; Theresa F. Latini, *The Church and the Crisis of Community: A Practical Theology of Small-group Ministry* (Grand Rapids, MI: Eerdmans 2011); Ronald J Lavin, *Way to Grow! Dynamic Church Growth Through Small Groups* (Lima, OH: CSS, 1996). Løvås, *Husmenigheten (The House Church)*. Magnus Malm, *Lille Vejledning Til Små Grupper [A Guide for Small Groups]* (Vejen: cBooks, 2009). Poole, *Seeker Small Groups*. Schilt, *Dynamic Small Groups*. Potter, *The Challenge of Cell Church*.

depth here. Some brief comments in the following paragraphs seem appropriate, however.

In a group that leads seekers towards faith, the first element of sharing and caring is a strong factor. It opens the way for life issues and the possibility of being vulnerable and honest. Related to the sharing is the second element: prayer for each other. God's blessings and guidance are asked on the issues that each person faces. Intercessory prayer will bring the members of the group together. Susanne and Cyril Kalvaag[51] point out that as the group experiences God's leading, faith grows in every member, but at a different pace and in different ways for each individual. Third, study and learning are important elements of the meetings, so that the group does not share only personal information and by so doing become introspective. There needs to be an inflow of information, teaching, and/or other input for the group members to feel that they are growing. Learning, in relationship to the issues the participants are talking about, is helpful. The content can include relational issues, social issues, and biblical materials, questions about spirituality or lifestyle. There is no particular limit to what the learning can be about as long as the group also remains focused on sharing, caring and praying.

The fourth element is doing something for other people outside the group. Some groups practice this by bringing new friends to the meetings in order to be of help to more people. Once the group has reached a certain sise, it splits into two and the process continues. Other groups set up a ministry to do some good in their local communities. This has proved helpful for several reasons. Working together for others creates joy and fellowship. Serving the community gives people a sense of being involved in Christian activity – of putting into practice the commandments of Jesus; it makes the Christian walk feel real. It also prevents the group from becoming too introverted. Those groups that have the same members for a long period of time

---

[51] Kalvaag and Kalvaag, The Café Church, Interview 1.

without any interaction with new people, tend to disintegrate and cease to operate. The last constituent of a successful small group is food. Eating together creates fellowship and openness. This aspect of evangelism is particularly emphasised in the Alpha-course, a program that was designed to bring basic Christian understanding to seekers and new believers. It is taken from the New Testament example of the early Christians eating together.

This chapter has looked at small groups in light of the conclusions drawn in chapter 7. Small groups seem to provide the type of forum people need in order to formulate their own faith and grow at their own speed under their own direction. Christian small groups which use the Bible as a reference point in an open exchange of ideas will help individuals to understand and reflect on Christian faith and yet remain in control of their own development. The characteristics of current Danish culture include individualism, a new approach to truth, a new spirituality and a changed relationship to groups and organisations. These can be handled well in the fellowship of a small group.

This study has described elements of the new culture the Danish Adventist Church operates within and also suggested ways for the church to respond. Establishing small groups for authentic, respectful and listening relationships creates a platform for spiritual growth. This implies a deep shift in church culture and I have no illusions as to the challenges that will come once these methods are introduced. In some respects these changes touch the Adventist Church at the core of its operation. The job description and score card for denominational workers will have to be adjusted, and following from that, changes in recruitment strategies and pastoral education will be called for. The administrative processes of the church will have to be adjusted and serious questions about the need for properties—and what kind of properties—will be asked. My current role in the education of workers for the church in Europe, lays a responsibility on me to prepare future ministers for the challenges the new spiritual climate brings to ministry and evangelism. An understanding of the new cultural context and a strategic approach working through networks and groups, church plants, pilot projects and new ministries is needed. Change is tough and the introduction of new methods will demand sacrifices. Still it is my conviction that if the Adventist Church wants to fulfil the commission of Jesus in Denmark today it will have to radically change its approach to ministry.

BIBLIOGRAPHY

Ahlin, Lars, *Pilgrim, Turist eller Flykting? en studie av individuell religiös rörlighet i senmoderniteten* (Stockholm: Östlings bokförlag Symposion, 2005)

_____, et al., 'Religious Diversity and Pluralism: Empirical Data and Theoretical Reflection from the Danish Pluralism Project', *Journal of Contemporary Religion,* 27:3 (October 2012), 403–18

Allan, J. A., 'The 'In Christ' Formula in Ephesians', *New Testament Studies,* 5 (1958), 54–61

Andersen, Peter B. (ed.), *Religion, Skole Og Kulturel Integration I Danmark Og Sverige* (Copenhagen: Museum Tusculanum, 2006)

Anderson, Ray Sherman, *An Emergent Theology for Emerging Churches* (Downers Grove, IL: InterVarsity Press, 2006)

Andreasen, Carl-David. '*Træk Fra Formandsrapporten*', *Adventnyt,* 96:7/8 (2004)

Arts, Wilhelmus Antonius, and Loek Halman, *European Values at the Turn of the Millennium* (Boston: Brill, 2004)

Aune, Kjell, A Contextual Analysis of the Seventh-Day Adventist Church in Norway: With Suggestions for Renewal and Growth, DMin Dissertation (Berrien Springs: Andrews University Theological Seminary, 2005)

Baumgartner, Erich Walter, *Re-Visioning Adventist Mission in Europe* (Berrien Springs, MI: Andrews University Press, 1998)

Bertens, Hans, *The Idea of the Postmodern: A History* (London: Routledge, 1994)

Billings, Bradley S., 'From House Church to Tenement Church', *Journal of Theological Studies,* 62:2 (2011), 541–69

Birch, Kenneth, '*Forvandling Og Fornyelse I Adventkirken*', *Adventnyt,* 102:6 (2010)

Birkedal, Erling, *Noen Ganger Tror Jeg På Gud, Men . . ?* (Trondheim: Forlaget Tapir, 2001)

Birley, Graham, and Neil Moreland, *A Practical Guide to Academic Research* (London: Kogan Page, 1998)

Bjerager, Erik, *Gud Bevare Danmark - et Opgør Med Secularismen* (Gylling: Gyldendal, 2006)

Bliss, Sylvester, *Memoirs of William Miller* (Berrien Springs, MI: Andrews University Press, 2005)

Bonhoeffer, Dietrich, *Life Together* (New York: Harper and Row, 1954)

Bouchet, Dominique, *Forandringer Af Betydning* (Aarhus: *Forlaget Afveje*, 2009)

Bruce, Steve, *God Is Dead: Secularisation in the West* (Oxford: Blackwell, 2002)

Bruinsma, Reinder, 'Adventist Identity in a Postmodern World', *Spectrum,* 41:2

(2013)

_____, *Faith Step by Step: Finding God and Yourself* (Grantham: Stanborough Press, 2006)

_____, *It's Time to Stop Rehearsing What We Believe & Start Looking at What Difference it Makes* (Nampa, ID: Pacific Press, 1998)

_____, 'Modern versus Postmodern Adventism: The Ultimate Divide?', *Ministry Magazine*, 77:6 (2005)

Brunstad, Paul Otto, *Ungdom Og Livstolkning* (Trondheim: Tapir forlag, 1998)

Bull, Malco and Keith Lockhart, *Seeking a Sanctuary: Seventh-Day Adventism and the American Dream* (Bloomington, IN: Indiana University Press, 2006)

Burrill, Russell, *Revolution in the Church* (Fallbrook, CA: Hart Research Center, 1993)

Caputo, John D., *What Would Jesus Deconstruct? The Good News of Postmodernism for the Church* (Grand Rapids, MI: Baker Academic, 2007)

Carson, D. A., *Becoming Conversant with the Emerging Church: Understanding a Movement and its Implications* (Grand Rapids, MI: Zondervan, 2005)

Christensen, Berit Schelde, Viggo Mortensen and Lars Buch Viftrup, *Karma, Koran Og Kirke; Religiøs Mangfoldighed Som Folkekirkelig Udfordring* (Højbjerg: Forlaget Univers, 2007)

Christoffersen, Lisbeth, Hans Raun Iversen, Niels Kærgård and Margit Warburg, *Fremtidens Danske Religionsmode* (Copenhagen: Forlaget Anis, 2012)

Connor, Steven, ed., *The Cambridge Companion to Postmodernism* (Cambridge: Cambridge University Press, 2004)

Cross, Whitney R., *The Burned-over District: Social and Intellectual History of Enthusiastic Religion in Western New York, 1800-50* (Ithaca, NY: Cornell University Press, 1981)

Damsteegt, P. Gerard, *Foundations of the Seventh-Day Adventist Message and Mission* (Berrien Springs, MI: Andrews University Press, 1995)

Davie, Grace, *Europe: The Exceptional Case* (London: Darton Longman & Todd, 2002)

Davie, Grace, Linda Woodhead and Paul Heelas, *Predicting Religion: Christian, Secular, and Alternative Futures* (Aldershot: Ashgate, 2003)

Dederen, Raoul, *Handbook of Seventh-Day Adventist Theology* (Hagerstown, MD: Review & Herald, 2000)

Donahue, Bill, *Building a Church of Small Groups: A Place Where Nobody Stands Alone* (Grand Rapids, MI: Zondervan, 2001)

Downing, Crystal, *How Postmodernism Serves (my) Faith: Questioning Truth in Language, Philosophy and Art* (Downers Grove, IL: InterVarsity Press, 2006)

Elkjær, Berit, '*Adventistkirken Åbner Genbrugsbutik På Nørrebro*', *Adventnyt*, 4 (2012), 5

_____, '*Verdens Bedste Missionsarbejde*', *Adventnyt*, 7/8 (2012), 4–5

Engen, Charles Edward (van), *God's Missionary People: Rethinking the Purpose of the Local Church* (Grand Rapids, MI: Baker Book House, 1991)

Ester, Peter, *The Individualizing Society* (Tilburg: Tilburg University Press, 1994)

Faddersbøll, Kurt, *Adventkirken Århus, Historie Og Begivenheder Gennem et Århundrede* (Århus: Private Publication, 1995)

Falk, Inger, '*Vi Elsker Fordi Han Elskede Først*', *Adventnyt*, 6 (2008), 7

Forhandlingsprotokol 30/5-80 for Syvende Dags Adventisternes Konferens I Danmark. Handwritten document. First Minutes, 30 May1880

Forhandlingsprotokol 30/6-86 for Syvende Dags Adventisternes Konferens I Danmark. Handwritten document, 30 June 1886

Forhandlingsprotokol 4/6-29 for Syvende Dags Advenntisternes Danske Konferens 1928 – 1937. Handwritten document, 4 June 1929

Forhandlingsprotokol24/9-81 for Syvende Dags Adventisternes Konferens I Danmark. Handwritten document, 4 September 1881

Forhandlingsprotokol28/6-28 for Syventde Dags Advenntisternes Danske Konferens 1928 – 1937. Handwritten document, Copenhagen, 28 June 1928

Franke, John R., *Manifold Witness - the Plurality of Truth* (Nashville, TN: Abingdon Press, 2009)

Froom, Leroy Edwin, *Movement of Destiny* (Washington, DC: Review & Herald, 1971)

Frost, Michael and Alan Hirsch, *The Shaping of Things to Come: Innovation and Mission for the 21st-Century Church* (Peabody, MA: Hendrickson, 2003)

Furseth, Inger, *From Quest for Truth to Being Oneself* (Frankfurt: Peter Lang, 2006)

Gallagher, Robert L. and Paul Hertig, *Mission in Acts: Ancient Narratives in Contemporary Context* (Maryknoll, NY: Orbis Books, 2004)

Galloway, Dale, *The Small Group Book* (Grand Rapids, MI: Revell, 1995)

Gibbs, Eddie, and Ryan Bolger, *Emerging Churches: Creating Christian Communities in Postmodern Cultures* (Grand Rapids, MI: Baker Academic, 2005)

Glasser, Arthur F., and Charles Edward van Engen, *Announcing the Kingdom: The Story of God's Mission in the Bible* (Grand Rapids, MI: Baker Academic, 2003)

Green, Joel B., *The Theology of the gospel of Luk,* (Cambridge: Cambridge University Press, 1995)

Green, Michael, *30 Years That Changed the World: A Fresh Look at the Book of Acts* (Leicester: InterVarsity Press, 2002)

Grenz, Stanley J., *A Primer on Postmodernism* (Grand Rapids, MI: Eerdmans, 1996)

Grenz, Stanley J., and Roger E. Olson, *Who Needs Theology? An Invitation to the Study of God* (Downers Grove, IL: InterVarsity Press, 1996)

Guder, Darrell L. et al., *Missional Church: A Vision for the Sending of the Church in North America* (Grand Rapids, MI: Eerdmans, 1998)

Gundelach, Peter, *Smaa og store Forandringer: Danskernes Værdier siden 1981* (Copenhagen: Hans Reitzels Forlag, 2011)

Gundelach, Peter, Hans Iversen and Margit Warburgh, *I hjertet af Danmark: institutioner og mentalitet,* (Copenhagen: Hans Reitzel, 2008)

Gustafsson, Göran, *Folkkyrkor Och Religiös Pluralism: Den Nordiska Religiösa Modellen* (Stockholm: Verbum, 2000)

Guthrie, Donald, *New Testament Introduction* (Leicester: InterVarsity Press, 1981)

Guy, Fritz, *Thinking Theologically: Adventist Christianity and the Interpretation of Faith* (Berrien Springs, MI: Andrews University Press, 1999)

Hammer, Olav, *På Jagt Efter Helheden: New Age - En Ny Folketro* (Aarhus: *Clemenstrykkeriet*, 1997)

Harper, Michael, *Let My People Grow: Ministry and Leadership in the Church* (London: Hodder and Stoughton, 1977)

Hastrup, Bjarne, *Verdens Danmark* (Copenhagen: Multivers, 2006)

Hearder, H., *Europe in the Nineteenth Century, 1830-1880* (Burnt Mill: Longman, 1988)

Heinz, Daniel, *Ludwig Richard Conradi: Missionar Evangelist Und Organisator Der Siebenten-Tags-Adventisten in Europa* (Frankfurt: Peter Lang, 1998)

Henderson, D. Michael, *A Model for Making Disciples: John Wesley's Class Meeting* (Napanee, IN: Evangel Publishing House, 2005)

Hewitt, Clyde E., *Midnight and Morning: An Account of the Adventist Awakening and the Founding of the Advent Christian Denomination, 1831-1860* (Charlotte, NC: Venture Books, 1983)

Hiebert, Paul G., *Anthropological Insights for Missionaries* (Grand Rapids, MI: Baker Academic, 1986)

_____. 'The Category 'Christian' in the Mission Task', *International Review of Mission*, 72 (1983), 421–27

Hirsch, Alan. *The Forgotten Ways: Reactivating the Missional Church* (Grand Rapids, MI: Brazos Press, 2006)

Hoehner, Harold W., *Ephesians: An Exegetical Commentary* (Grand Rapids, MI: Baker Academic, 2002)

Holloway, Immy, *Qualitative Research in Health Care* (Maidenhead: Open University Press, 2005)

Howell, Emma E., *Den Store Adventbevegelsen*, (Oslo: Skandinavisk Bogforlag, n. d.)

Hunter, George G., *How to Reach Secular People* (Nashville, TN: Abingdon Press, 1992)

Hybels, Bill, 'From Here to There', (Willow Creek: Willow Creek Association UK and Ireland, 2010)

Jakobsen, Merete D., 'Power of the Spirits: Spirituality in Denmark', *Shaman: An International Journal for Shamanistic Research*, 14 (2006), 9–17

Jensen, Sven Hagen. 'Historie - KS', (6 June 2013)

Jones, A.T., 'Missionaries for God', *General Conference Bulletin* 2 (First Quarter 1897)

Jørgensen, Kenneth, '*Mod Høst 90* (Harvest 90)', *Adventnyt*, 81:3 (1989)

Keel, Tim, *Intuitive Leadership: Embracing a Paradigm of Narrative, Metaphor, and Chaos* (Grand Rapids, MI: Baker Books, 2007)

Kent Kingston, 'A Fresh Vision of Church', *Adventist Record*, (5 April 2014), 14–15

Kirkpatrick, Thomas G., *Small Groups in the Church: A Handbook for Creating Communit*, (Bethesda, MD: Alban Institute, 1995)

Knight, George R., *A Brief History of Seventh-Day Adventists* (Hagerstown, MD: Review & Herald, 2012)

_____, *A Search For Identity: The Development of Seventh-Day Adventist Beliefs Edition* (Hagerstown, MD: Review & Herald, 2000)

_____, *William Miller and the Rise of Adventism*, (Nampa, ID: Pacific Press, 2011)

Kolind, Lars, *Vidensamfundet* (Copenhagen: Gyldendal, 2001)

Kotter, John P. and Dan S. Cohen, *The Heart of Change* (Boston: Harvard Business School Press, 2002)

_____, *A Force for Change: How Leadership Differs from Management* (New York: The Free Press, 1990)

_____, *Leading Change* (Boston, MA: Harvard Business Review Press, 2012)

Kvinge, Rolf, '*København for Kristus*', *Adventnyt*, 81:4 (1989)

Ladd, George Eldon, *A Theology of the New Testament* (Grand Rapids, MI: Eerdmans, 1974)

Lehmann, Richard, Jack Mahon and Borge Schantz, eds., *Cast the Net on the Right Side: Seventh-Day Adventists Face the "Isms,"* (Bracknell: European Institute of World Mission, 1993)

Lewis, A. H., 'From Brother Lewis', *Advent Review and Sabbath Herald*, 13:11 (3 February 1959), 8

Lewis, Robert, Wayne Cordeiro and Warren Bird, *Culture Shift: Transforming Your Church from the Inside Out* (San Francisco: John Wiley & Sons, 2005)

Liamputtong, Pranee, *Focus Group Methodology: Principle and Practice* (London: SAGE, 2011)

Liefeld, Walter L., *Ephesians* (Downers Grove, IL: InterVarsity Press, 1997)

Lyons, Gabe, *The Next Christians* (Colorado Springs, CO: Multnomah, 2012)

Mallison, John, *Small Group Leader: A Manual to Develop Vital Small Groups* (Bletchley: Scripture Union Publishing, 1996)

Malpas, Simon, *The Postmodern* (Milton Park: Routledge, 2005)

Mann, Alice, *Can Our Church Live? Redeveloping Congregations in Decline* (New York: Alban Institute, 2000)

Martin, David, *Religious and the Secular* (London: Routledge & Kegan Paul PLC, 1969)

Matteson, John, *Mattesons Liv Og Adventbevægelsens Begyndelse Blandt Skandinaverne,* (College View, NE: International Publishing, 1908)

Maxwell, C. Mervyn, *Tell It to the World* (Boise, ID: Pacific Press, 1998)

Maxwell, John C., *The 21 Irrefutable Laws of Leadership* (Nashville, TN: Thomas Nelson, 1998)

McBride, Neal, *How to Build a Small Groups Ministry* (Colorado Springs, CO: NavPress, 1995)

McNeal, Reggie, *Missional Renaissance: Changing the Scorecard for the Church* (San Francisco: Jossey-Bass, 2009)

_____, *The Present Future: Six Tough Questions for the Church,*(San Fransisco: Jossey Bass, 2003)

Metzger, Bruce M., Michael David Coogan, *The Oxford Companion to the Bible* (New York: Oxford University Press, 1993)

'Missionsefterretninger', *Missionefterretninger,* (10 October 1934)

Mortensen, Viggo, *Kristendommen under Forvandling* (Højbjerg: Forlaget Univers, 2005)

_____, (ed.) *Er Kristendommen under Forvandling?* (Højbjerg: Forlaget Univers, 2005)

Muddiman, John, *The Epistle to the Ephesians: A Commentary* (London: Continuum, 2001)

Müller, Andreas, '*Happy Hand Udvider I Aalborg*', *Adventnyt,* 2 (2014), 7

Müller, Anne-May, '*Det Er Koldt at Være Due*', *Adventnyt,* 4 (2005), 12–13

Murray, Stuart, *Church after Christendom* (Milton Keynes: Paternoster, 2004)

Nielsen, Line, 'Rejsen Sammen', Http://adventist.dk/da/faellesskab/arsmode-generalforsamling-2013/sagspapir. *Generalforsamling 2013*, June 2013

Nielsen Ravnkilde and Kurt Ravnkilde, '*Knæfald for Ungdommen*', Adventnyt, 96:12 (2004), 14

Nouwen, Henry, *Creative Ministry* (New York: Bantam, Doubleday, Dell, 1978)

Osmer, Richard Robert, *Practical Theology: An Introduction* (Grand Rapids, MI: Eerdmans, 2008)

Paulien, Jon, *Everlasting gospel, Ever-Changing World: Introducing Jesus to a Skeptical Generation* (Nampa, ID: Pacific Press, 2008)

Peck, Adrian, *Church Growth In Britain: A Thematic Analysis of Two Growing British Churches*, MA Dissertation (Binfield: Newbold College of Higher Education 2014)

Pedersen, Kaj, *Syvende Dags Adventistkirken I Danmark* (Copenhagen: Dansk Bogforlag, 2007)

Pedersen, Rene D., 'The Second Golden Age of Theosophy in Denmark: An Existential 'Template' for Late Modernity?', *Aries*, 9.2 (2009), 233–62

'Planer for Evangelisme'. *Missionsefterretninger Fra Norge Og Danmark, Stories from the Mission Work in Denmark and Norway* (10 October 1928)

Poole, Garry, *Seeker Small Groups: Engaging Spiritual Seekers in Life-Changing Discussions* (Grand Rapids, MI: Zondervan : Willow Creek Resources, 2003)

Pujic, Miroslav, 'Postmodern Cultural Patterns', *Ministry Magazine*, 85:6 (June 2013), 32

_____, and Sarah K. Asaftei, *Experiencing the Joy* (St. Albans: LIFEdevelopment Discipleship library, 2012)

Qvortrup Fibiger, Marianne C., 'The Danish Pluralism Project', *Religion*, 39:2 (2009), 169–75

Raport Fra Syvende Dags Adventisternes Øst-Danske Konferens. Handwritten document. Suomis vej 5, Copenhagen, August 1936

Report from the Scandinavian Union; *Missionsefterretninger Fra Norge Og Danmark, Stories from the Mission Work in Denmark and Norway* (9 September 1928)

Rice, Richard, *Reign of God: An Introduction to Christian Theology from a Seventh-Day Adventist Perspective* (Berrien Springs, MI: Andrews University Press, 1997)

Rolf Gustafson, *Tid För Dialog* (Uppsala: Trotts Allt, 1994)

Roulund-Nørgaard, Søren, *Gør danerne kristne: DAWN rapporten* (Lemvig: SALT, 1992)

Saarinen, Martin F., *The Life Cycle of a Congregation* (New York: Alban Institute, 1998)

Schantz, Børge, and Reinder Bruinsma, *Exploring the Frontiers of Faith, Festschrift in Honour of Dr. Jan Paulsen* (Lueneburg: Advent-Verlag, 2009)

Schantz, Hans Jørgen, *I Troens Bakspejl* (Copenhagen: Dansk Bogforlag, 1998)

Schwarz, Richard W., *Light Bearers to the Remnant* (Mountain View, CA: Pacific Press, 1979)

'Sine Renlev', HASDA, historical archives of the Seventh-day Adventist Church in Denmark, 1999.

Sjöborg, Anders, *Bibeln På Mina Egna Villkor*, Acta Universitatis Upsaliensis (Uppsala: Uppsala University Library i distr., 2006)

'Skolens Historie', Http://www.xn--jf-lka.dk/index.php/skolen. *Østervrå-Jerslev Friskole*, n.d.

Smith, James K. A., *Who's Afraid of Postmodernism? Taking Derrida, Lyotard, and Foucault to Church* (Grand Rapids, MI: Baker Academic, 2006)

Stott, John, *Christian Mission in the Modern World* (London: Falcon, 1975)

_____, *The Message of Ephesians: God's New Society* (Leicester: InterVarsity Press, 1989)

Strobel, Lee, *Inside the Mind of Unchurched Harry & Mary: How to Reach Friends and Family Who Avoid God and the Church* (Grand Rapids, MI: Zondervan, 1993)

Stumpf, Hans, 'A Visit to an Adventist Café Church', *Adventnyt*, 97:6 (2005)

Sutcliffe, Steven and Marion Bowman, *Beyond New Age: Exploring Alternative Spirituality* (Edinburgh: Edinburgh University Press, 2000)

Swinton, John, and Harriet Mowat, *Practical Theology and Qualitative Research* (London: SCM, 2006)

'The European Social Study', Http://www.europeansocialsurvey.org/about/index.html. *About ESS*, 9 April 2014

'The European Values Study', Http://www.europeanvaluesstudy.eu/, 10 August 2013

Verhey, Allen, and Joseph S. Harvard, *Ephesians* (Louisville, KY: Westminster/John Knox, 2011)

Verrecchia, Jean-Claude. *God of No Fixed Address. From Altars to Sanctuaries, Temples to Houses* (Eugene, OR: Wipf & Stock, 2015)

Walshe, Allan Roy, *A Paradigm Shift: Moving from an Informational to a Relational Model of Ministry in the Adventist Churches of New Zealand*, DMin Dissertation (Pasadena, CA: Fuller Theological Seminary, 2007)

White, Ellen G. *Ellen G White Manuscript Releases,* Vol. 19 (Silver Spring, MA: Ellen G. White Estate, 1990)

_____, *Christian Experience and Teaching of Ellen G. White* (Mountain View, CA: Pacific Press, 1940)

_____, *Education* (Mountain View, CA: Pacific Press, 1952)

_____, *gospel Workers* (Washington, DC: Review & Herald, 1948)

_____, *Historical Sketches of the Foreign Missions of the Seventh-Day Adventists*, (Basel: Imprimerie Polyglotte, 1886)

_____, *Ministry of Healing*, (Mountain View, CA: Pacific Press, 1942)

_____, 'Cooperation with God and Fellow Workers Necessary for Success in Fulfilling gospel Commission', Manuscript Released No. 1230, Ellen G. White Estate (Washington, DC, 23 January 1987)

_____, *Spirit of Prophecy,* Vol. 4 (Oakland, CA: Pacific Press, 1884)

_____, *Testimonies for the Church,* Vol. 7 (Mountain View, CA: Pacific Press, 1948)

_____, *The Acts of the Apostles* (Mountain View, CA: Pacific Press, 1911)

_____, *The Colporteur Evangelist*, 1st ed. (Mountain View, CA: Pacific Press, n.d.)

_____, *The Great Controversy* (Mountain View, CA: Pacific Press, 1907)

_____, *The Ministry Of Healing* (Mountain View, CA: Pacific Press, 1942)

White, James, 'The Conference Address',*Review & Herald,* 41:23 (May 20 1873), 8

Wiik, Betina, 'Personal Statement', *Adventnyt,* 98:5 (2006), 23

Williams, David J., *Acts - New International Biblical Commentary New Testament 5*. Subsequent edition (Peabody, MA: Hendrickson, 2002)

Willis, Jerry, *Foundations of Qualitative Research: Interpretive and Critical Approaches* (Thousand Oaks, CA: SAGE, 2007)

Working Policy of the General Conference of the Seventh-day Adventist Church, 2010-2011 Edition (Hagerstown, MD: Review & Herald, 2010).

www.ingramcontent.com/pod-product-compliance
Lightning Source LLC
Chambersburg PA
CBHW051944290426
44110CB00015B/2103